REVOLU-TION IN CENTRAL AMERICA

GLENN ALAN CHENEY

A GROLIER COMPANY

FRANKLIN WATTS
NEW YORK | LONDON | TORONTO | SYDNEY | 1984
AN IMPACT BOOK

Map by Vantage Art, Inc.

Photographs courtesy of
UPI: pp. 20, 28, 31, 46, 51, 54, 67, 70, 82.

Library of Congress Cataloging in Publication Data

Cheney, Glenn Alan.
Revolution in Central America.

(An Impact book)
Includes index.
Summary: Explores the causes of conflict in Central
America, examining the social-political-historical elements
of each country individually in its struggle for change.
1. Central America—History—Juvenile literature.
2. Revolutions—Central America—Juvenile literature.
3. Central America—Foreign relations—United States—
Juvenile literature. 4. United States—Foreign relations
—Central America—Juvenile literature. [1. Central
America—History. 2. Revolutions—Central America]
I. Title. II. Series
F1428.5.C48   1984   972.8   83-23394
ISBN 0-531-04761-X

CONTENTS

TO
RALPH ALBERT CHENEY
AND
RUTH REES CHENEY

REVOLUTION IN
CENTRAL AMERICA

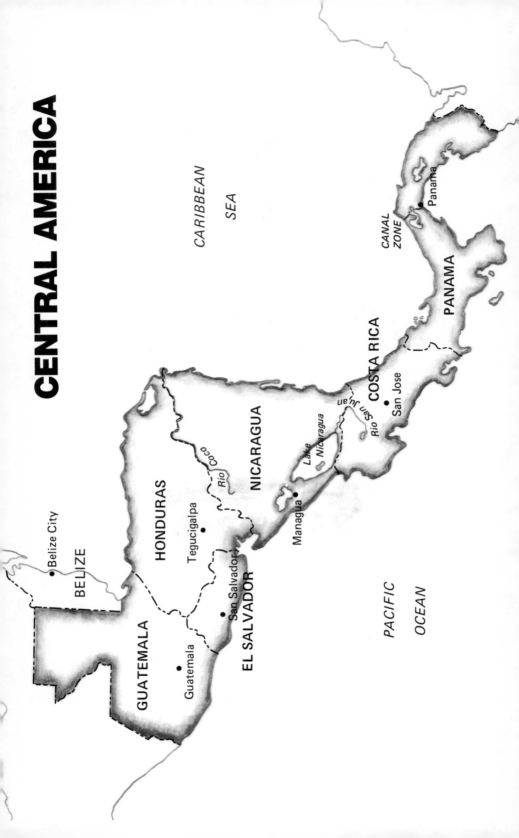

CENTRAL AMERICA

CARIBBEAN

SEA

PACIFIC

OCEAN

• Belize City

BELIZE

GUATEMALA

• Guatemala

EL SALVADOR

• San Salvador

HONDURAS

• Tegucigalpa

Rio Coco

NICARAGUA

• Managua

Lake Nicaragua

Rio San Juan

COSTA RICA

• San Jose

CANAL ZONE

PANAMA

• Panama

INTRODUCTION

Revolution in Central America is a product of the region's past. Since the early years of this century, the people of Nicaragua, El Salvador, Honduras, and Guatemala have been suffering widespread poverty, hunger, disease, illiteracy, and political repression. Military governments have prohibited the democratic processes that might have alleviated some of these problems. As the suffering became intolerable, rebellion became inevitable.

The recent insurgencies of Central America have not been completely spontaneous, however. The Soviet Union and Cuba have contributed weapons, training, advice, and encouragement to guerrilla armies. The United States has responded by offering similar aid to anticommunist governments, and by trying to develop democracies and encourage social reforms intended to cure the fundamental causes of revolution. As East meets West on the battlefields of Central America, the conflicts take on global proportions.

The situation is not simple. Each country has unique problems. Nicaragua, having already overthrown a corrupt dictator, replacing him with a government backed by Cuba, is under attack by counterrevolutionaries backed by the United States. El Salvador, torn between rebellious guerrillas and brutal military forces, has a new and very fragile democracy. Guatemala, which has not had an honestly elected government survive a full term in over 100 years, has been the scene of horrendous massacres as the military wipes out entire villages to deny rebel guerrillas the support they need to survive. Honduras, the poorest country in the region, with a shaky, new democracy, has miraculously escaped widespread insurgency. But it has become involved with the counterrevolutionary invasion of Nicaragua and is on the brink of war with that country. Only Costa Rica, the region's sole democracy, is free of violent conflict.

President Ronald Reagan has stated that the future of Central America is crucial to the security of the United States. What, then, is the proper response to rebel forces that denounce U.S. "imperialism" while accepting arms and advice from the Soviet Union? How much military support should the United States contribute to uphold the struggling, newborn democracies of El Salvador and Honduras? How actively should the United States oppose the Soviet-backed government of Nicaragua? Are there any peaceful solutions to the civil wars in Central America?

The problems of Central America are as complex as international politics and as simple as hungry stomachs. Only through an understanding of these problems can we hope to find their solutions. The lives of as many as 100,000 or more people, as well as the security of the United States and the rest of Latin America, are at stake.

THE STRUGGLE TOWARD CHANGE

There are two widely debated explanations for the causes of conflict in Central America. One is rooted in four centuries of history; the other blames the East-Western political struggles between the two super-powers: the United States and the Soviet Union. Neither explanation alone is correct. The problems are caused by a combination of factors.

From the historical perspective Central America, like most of Latin America, has lagged behind the social and political developments that have taken place in more advanced countries. Industrialization, democracy, the development of a middle class—these modern concepts have not become reality in most Central American countries. Socially, there is still a sharp division between the very rich upper class and the very poor lower class. Politically, the leaders of these countries have been dictators who have used military strength to secure their office and prevent uprisings of the lower class.

From the perspective of modern politics, Latin America has become a focal point of the East's and the West's efforts to spread their spheres of influence as widely as possible. While the Soviet Union is trying to win or create allies in Central America, the United States feels threatened by Soviet-backed countries so close to U.S. borders. With both sides trying to exert influence over more governments, people, and territory, there is partial truth in the claim that Central American blood is being shed in a conflict between two foreign powers.

To understand the situation in Central America, it is necessary to look at both the overall historical and the political perspectives. Only then can we analyze the situation in each individual country.

HISTORICAL PERSPECTIVE

Today's problems in Central America can be traced back to the arrival of the Spanish *conquistadores* in the early sixteenth century. Unlike the colonizers of North America, who came to start a new life and build a new society, the conquerors of Central America came to exploit the New World and carry its riches back to Spain. The new North Americans, coming from England, where commerce was well established and the principles of democracy were developing, built their society on the foundations of liberty and free enterprise. The new Latin Americans, however, came from a country where kings still ruled a feudalistic society of serfs and overlords.

Naturally the colonizers of Central America based their New World society on the feudalism of Spain. At the top of the social structure were a few wealthy families of royal birth who owned most of the land. Most other people either were in the army or were peasant sharecroppers who rented their tiny plots of land and gave their landlords portions of their harvests in payment. With no middle class between the rich and the poor, there was little possibility that these peasants, the *campesinos*, could ever improve their position in the socioeconomic scale.

In 1821, all of Central America from Panama to Mexico became a single independent country called the Federation of Central America. Slavery was abolished in 1824. Although the power and wealth that came with Spanish royalty were no longer a birthright, the wealthy landowners retained control over the government and remained at the top of the socioeconomic structure. They were an oligarchy—a small group of rulers whose wealth and political power stayed in the same families for generations.

Feudalism was still the basic social order, but some landowners thought the former colonies were ready to mature into a system more like the democratic, capitalistic nations of North America. These landowners who wanted to change the political order were called liberals. Those who wanted to retain the old system were called conservatives. Local battles between the two, fought by drafted *campesinos* who had little to gain from a victory by either side, kept the region in political chaos. In 1838, the Federation broke up into six countries: Panama, Costa Rica, El Salvador, Honduras, Guatemala, and Mexico.

Exept for a few instances of honest elections, dictators controlled the governments of these countries. Much of the territory in each country, however, was ruled by powerful landowners or gang leaders, called *caudillos*, who effectively determined the law in their own areas. These *caudillos* kept their own security forces, appointed their own judges, and used their wealth to maintain control over local army commanders. The *campesinos* who rented or worked on the *caudillos'* land had few rights, since there was no police force or judicial system for them to appeal to for help.

THE STRUGGLE TO CHANGE

Central American feudalism, *caudillos*, and an oligarchic social structure have survived well into the twentieth century. Until very recently, people who inherited land and wealth still ruled above the law in their own territories. Governments were still led by dictators, and local security forces were still controlled by local landowners. Peasants had few rights and little hope of gaining wealth. A tiny portion of the population was fabulously rich while the vast masses lived in utter, inescapable poverty. Well into the twentieth century, much of Central America was politically, socially, and economically still in the sixteenth century. But the situation has begun to change.

This change, however, is coming through violent conflict. As in the past, the battle is between liberals and conservatives, though their beliefs have changed with the times. The conservatives of today, also called *rightists*, are generally the wealthy, landed oligarchy and those loyal to it. They do not want a democracy that would threaten their power, or a more even distribution of wealth that would threaten their standard of living. They are considered capitalists because they want to preserve the right of private property and especially their possession of it.

Today's liberals, also referred to as *leftists*, are generally those who want a change to either a democracy or a hard-line Marxist government that will take the land and wealth from the oligarchy and distribute them among the poor. Many, though by no means all, leftists are of the middle and lower class, that is, those who have little opportunity to better their lives unless the political and economic system is changed. Few of the poor people in the lower class understand Marxism, but they are often called communists because they want to reorganize the socioeconomic structure of their countries by taking some of the wealth and power from the upper class and distributing them among the poor. In some cases, moderate leftists simply want their governments to respect basic human rights. More extreme leftists want to install a communist regime that will outlaw private property so that "the people" as a whole own all farms and industries. Others, angry about the corruption and abuse of human rights in their governments, simply want to tear down one government and replace it with another.

THE ROLE OF THE CHURCH

The Roman Catholic Church has always been a powerful influence in Latin America. Priests arrived with the *conquistadores* and attempted to convert the Indians, who were being slaughtered, tortured, or sold as slaves. The Church soon became the largest landowner and thus the wealthiest institution in Latin America. As the allegedly infallible leader of virtually 100 percent of the population, the Church was also a politically powerful organization.

Until the 1960s, the Church used its unquestioned influence to preserve the social and political system that kept the oligarchy in power and the masses in silent misery. Intellectuals said that one priest could keep more order than a dozen of the *caudillo's* henchmen. By preaching that poverty was good for the soul, that violence, even against an oppressor, was sinful, and that everything existed just as God willed it, priests taught the poor to passively accept their fate.

The Church began a radical shift in policy and attitude during the 1960s. Papal encyclicals in 1961, 1963, and 1965 declared everyone's right to education, decent living conditions, and political freedom. In

1968, at the second Latin American Episcopal Conference in Medellin, Colombia, the Church took a stance that finally broke up the 300-year-old alliance between the church and the oligarchy. The bishops at the meeting denounced "institutionalized violence" and the "international imperialism of money" and committed the Church to the salvation of the oppressed and the downtrodden.

The Medellin conference inspired many priests, and even some bishops and archbishops, to adopt the so-called Theology of Liberation. They went further than just helping the poor better their living standards. They became actively involved in politics and even in armed rebellion. When these clergymen tried to make the illiterate *campesinos* conscious of the social, economic, and political injustices that kept them in poverty and misery, the oligarchy declared them "leftist subversives" who were undermining the foundations of society as it had stood for three centuries. The efforts of priests and churchworkers to mobilize the poor only brought more repression from rightists, who used force to prevent change. As it became apparent that only force could defeat force, many priests gave moral sanction to the leftists who took up arms in rebellion. A few priests even gave up the priesthood to join guerrilla armies.

THE ROLE OF
THE SOVIET BLOC

One of the most basic debates over Central America today is about the cause of its several rebellions. Are they arising spontaneously from the miserable conditions of poverty and repression, or is the fighting being instigated and continued by communist subversives trained and armed by the Soviet Union and its allies?

Communism first established itself in the western hemisphere when leftist guerrillas led by Fidel Castro overthrew the rightist government of Cuba in 1959. After promises of elections and a free enterprise system, Castro nationalized all industries and farms, arrested or executed all political opposition, eliminated most political rights, and without benefit of elections assumed the position of head of state. He has ruled unchallenged ever since.

With strong backing from the Soviet Union, Castro's admitted objective has been to spread communist revolution across Latin America, to "liberate" the impoverished masses from the oppression of their governments and to break the economic grip of the "Yanqui (Yankee) imperialists."

Evidence of Cuban involvement in Central American politics and revolution has been overwhelming. Many guerrillas from Nicaragua, El Salvador, Honduras, and Guatemala have received training in Cuba. A few have even traveled to the Soviet Union. Arms from Soviet-bloc countries around the world have passed through Cuba on their way to the isthmus.

In May 1983, the U.S. State and Defense Departments released a report entitled, "Background Paper: Central America." The report portrayed Cuba as playing a major role in every rebellion in the region. It claimed that Cuba cooperated with the Soviet military, the KGB, the Palestinian Liberation Organization, and Libya to supply training, arms, and moral support to guerrillas. Outlining Cuba's strategies, the report explained that Cuba had helped unify various leftist factions in different countries, provided hundreds of tons of arms and ammunition to guerrillas, and started a communist party and guerrilla group in Latin America's oldest democracy, Costa Rica.

The report also alleged that Cuba had used propaganda to create an image of the guerrillas as liberators and to foster international support for them. Tactics included the constant repetition that the rebellions were "people's" revolutions, the enlisting of the political and moral support of countries all over the world, the strengthening of ties with as many American organizations as possible, and the use of humanitarian organizations for financial support of the revolutions.

U.S. CONCERNS

In October 1962, the United States discovered that the Soviet Union was installing nuclear missiles in Cuba, just 90 miles (145 km) from the U.S. mainland. President John F. Kennedy demanded that the missiles be removed. Soviet Premier Nikita Krushchev refused. During a very tense week, the two countries bordered on war until Krushchev backed down and removed the missiles. The United States, although relieved, realized the danger of communist-controlled countries so close to home.

The danger today is not of missiles but of spreading communist influence in Latin America. Many Americans are concerned about the so-called domino theory, which predicts that if one country falls to invasion or revolution, its neighbors will soon suffer the same fate. The neighbors of those countries will fall as well, and the process will continue with the countries falling like dominoes toppling down in a row. If the domino theory is valid, then the conflicts in Central America could be just the beginning of many revolutions all over Latin America.

Central America is not so far from the United States. El Salvador, for example, is closer to Houston, Texas than Houston is to Washington, D.C., a fact that means communist uprisings in the region are quite literally in the backyard of the United States. Americans have reason to be concerned about the security of their own country as well as that of their neighbors to the south.

If Latin America became overwhelmingly pro-Soviet and anti-American, the United States would face several problems. The sea lanes of the Panama Canal, the Caribbean, and parts of the Atlantic and Pacific Oceans would be jeopardized. The natural resources of Latin America, which include bountiful deposits of oil, iron, bauxite, copper, tin, gold, silver, and many other essential natural resources, might not be as readily or as inexpensively available to the United States. At the same time, American manufacturers might lose easy access to the Latin American market for their goods. There is also the probability that millions of Hispanic refugees would flee communist regimes and arrive in the United States with neither money nor the means of supporting themselves.

The same conditions that breed revolt in Central America—totalitarian governments, poverty, and illiteracy—are common throughout Latin America. It is therefore of utmost importance that the United States find solutions to the problems of Central America that can be applied in other countries before they, too, become entangled in civil wars.

While they have many problems in common, the countries of Central America are each in a unique situation. Before we can find solutions to their problems, we have to understand their individual situations. Only then can we move toward the peace crucial to the future of the United States and Latin America.

NICARAGUA

Internal turmoil is nothing new to Nicaragua. After the arrival of the Spanish *conquistadores*, conservative and liberal *caudillos* fought almost unending civil wars over boundaries, access to rivers and roads, political office, and the laws that would govern their local areas. Wealth and power were traded back and forth among the *caudillos*, but little trickled down to the *campesinos*, whose fate remained in the hands of the upper class.

AN OMINOUS BEGINNING

After Nicaragua became an independent country in 1838, the conservative-liberal contest there became an all-out civil war. An American transport company that shipped goods and people by land across the Central American isthmus from the Atlantic to the Pacific wanted a liberal government that would encourage capitalism and allow the company to continue its business. The firm hired an American soldier-of-fortune, William Walker, to support the liberals with a force of American mercenaries. He did so, defeating the conservatives in 1855. But he then went on to overthrow the liberal leaders, and in a fraudulent election in 1856, he became president of Nicaragua.

Walker, who came from the American South, reintroduced slavery in Nicaragua and began plans to conquer and unite Central America. Forces from neighboring countries, foreseeing trouble, invaded Nicaragua and ousted Walker. He arrived in New York a hero, recruited a small army there, and returned to Central America. After taking a small town in Honduras, he was captured and executed. It was a dark beginning for the next 120 years of relations between the United States and Nicaragua.

THREE AMERICAN INVASIONS

Toward the end of the nineteenth century, coffee became a highly profitable crop. Until then, most Nicaraguan farmers had grown only what they themselves needed to eat. Now the government, hoping to bring more money into the country, wanted the farmers to grow coffee as a cash crop that could be sold and exported. During a sixteen-year liberal presidency, several unfair laws forced the subsistence farmers to sell their small plots of land to plantation owners who would grow coffee. Other laws forced the unemployed to accept low-paying work on these plantations.

When the United States began construction of the Panama Canal in 1903, Nicaragua announced intentions of building its own canal with the help of Germany and Japan. The United States, wanting neither foreign influence in the Americas nor competition for its expensive new canal, sent the U.S. Marines to aid an uprising of conservatives in 1909. The Nicaraguan government was overthrown, and the conservative rebel leader who became president allowed U.S. representatives to control most industries and government functions—everything from the post office and customs houses to the banks, mines, and railroads. For the next twenty-five years, Nicaragua seemed more like an American state than an independent country.

Nevertheless, unrest was never far beneath the surface. In 1912, a troop of 2,700 Marines again landed in Nicaragua to suppress a national uprising. Even after order was restored, a detachment of Marines remained until 1925. Then two months after they had left, the Marines were called back to stop yet another civil war. Again they remained, this time to battle Central America's first communist revolutionaries.

SANDINO VS. SOMOZA: NICARAGUA'S FIRST GUERRILLA WAR

In 1926, a young Nicaraguan named Augusto César Sandino returned from Mexico with ideas about communism, which he advocated, and foreign imperialism, which he denounced. The imperialists were the Americans, whose military forces, Sandino felt, did not belong in Nicaragua. He led a small band of guerrillas in sneak attacks against the Nicaraguan government and the U.S. Marines. The Marines suffered enough casualties that Americans began protesting, shouting "U.S. out of Nicaragua"—not unlike the demands of their grandchildren over a similar situation in Vietnam some forty years later. In the face of opposition at home, the Marines created, trained, and armed the Nicaraguan National Guard to continue the fight. Against the judgment of Nicaragua's president, they made Anastasio "Tacho" Somoza chief of this new security force.

Somoza had built a reputation as a businessman who led several companies into bankruptcy and used forgery and counterfeiting to pay bad debts he had acquired through excessive gambling. But he had married into a good family and knew enough to please the American allies, who, recent history had shown, held the real reins of power in Nicaragua.

With ruthless severity, Somoza's National Guard wiped out Sandino's forces, carelessly killing thousands of civilians in the process. Somoza then returned to the capital, Managua, to oust the president and seize control of the country.

THE SOMOZA DYNASTY

Somoza immediately began pillaging his country. Using the strength of his office, he bought up huge tracts of land. He collected taxes on illegal trades such as prostitution and gambling. He was known to be receiving $400,000 per year in payoffs from foreign companies that needed his government's cooperation. He treated the Nicaraguan treasury as his personal checking account.

In 1956, Anastasio Somoza was assassinated. His eldest son Luis assumed the presidency, behaving just as his father had. When he died in 1967, Luis was replaced by his brother, Anastasio "Tachito" Somoza Debayle. The government continued as before. Corruption was not a crime as much as a standard way of running the country and its businesses. By 1979, the Somoza family owned 77,000 square miles (200,000 km) of the best coffee, cotton, and cattle land as well as estates in Costa Rica, Mexico, and the United States. Tens of millions of dollars were stashed in foreign banks. Virtually every important industry and business in Nicaragua was owned or controlled by a Somoza.

Discontent with this government was deep and widespread, cutting across class lines. The lower class, about two-thirds of Nicaragua's three million people, had no hope of escaping poverty because the government provided few schools, little medical care, and not much chance of holding on to any farmland a Somoza might want to buy. The middle class, less than a third of the population, had little chance to improve its lot because the Somozas had sapped the economy so badly that there were few government services and the development of business was virtually impossible. And the upper class felt paralyzed because no major investments were possible without the political support of the ruling family. The Somozas owned so much of so many different industries—especially those relating to agriculture—that no one could carry on business without their cooperation, which was available only for a price.

Opposition to the Somoza style of government was dangerous. The National Guard, still operating as the private militia of the president, had little regard for constitutional law. Anyone speaking out against the government was arrested or simply shot on sight. Elections were hardly valid because only those who voted for Somoza's party received special red identity cards. Without this card, one could not get a job, a passport, or any favor or service from the government.

THE SANDINISTA REVOLUTION

During the 1970s, discontent grew into violent restlessness. When an earthquake destroyed Managua in 1972, killing 10,000 and leaving 200,000 homeless, the emergency aid from other countries ended up in the pockets of Anastasio Somoza Debayle and his brother. Years later, much of the capital was still in ruins. This convinced a large portion of the Nicaraguan people that their government was truly against them. Several weak political parties joined with labor unions to demand a move toward democracy. At the same time a small guerrilla group named after Augusto Sandino, the Sandinista National Liberation Front (or FSLN, from its Spanish initials), gained popular support and began daring kidnappings of government officials and raids on isolated National Guard outposts. The government labeled the guerrillas "communists," but the Sandinistas maintained that they were simply against the Somoza regime and in favor of social justice and democracy.

In November 1977, *La Prensa*, the only Nicaraguan newspaper that had ever dared to criticize the government, published a full-page appeal for democracy that was signed by twelve economic, cultural, and religious leaders. Three months later, the editor of *La Prensa*, Pedro Joaquín Chamorro, was assassinated by a rightist death squad.

The murder, obviously committed with consent of the government, was the final act that turned almost the entire population against Anastasio "Tachito" Somoza Debayle. Some 120,000 people attended Chamorro's funeral. A nationwide labor strike in protest was joined by workers and management alike. Somoza's attempts to buy back their support with wage increases, bonuses, and other concessions were unsuccessful.

In August 1978, guerrilla leader Edén Pastora Gomez, known then only as "Commander Zero," and a band of FSLN commandos took over the National Palace, capturing 500 top government officials. The captives were freed in exchange for $5 million, the release of eighty-three political prisoners, and safe passage to Panama. The courageous raid not only succeeded in raising money and freeing prisoners but also brought worldwide attention to the growing opposition of the Somoza regime.

Two months later, Edén Pastora launched the Sandinista invasion from Costa Rica. Its advance was gradual but persistent. Virtually the entire population supported it, as did most other Central American countries. The National Guard was under constant attack from all sides, by everyone from well-trained guerrillas with modern weapons to young children with rocks and slingshots. Unlike the National Guard, the guerrillas were careful to respect not only Nicaraguan civilians, but also foreign journalists who were reporting on the war. This gave the guerrillas the support of their own people and that of people all over the world.

Having nothing to lose personally by holding out, Somoza ordered a fight to the finish. The National Guard slaughtered tens of thousands of civilians. Planes bombed residential neighborhoods without reason. The only farms and factories that escaped destruction were those owned by Somozas. The president did not flee until a few hours before his bunker at the National Palace was surrounded by the FSLN on July 19, 1979. Leaving behind 50,000 dead and a country completely in ruins, Somoza lived in the United States and then in Paraguay until Sandinista commandos with bazookas ambushed his car in 1980.

During the final year of heavy fighting, President Somoza was pleading for military aid from the United States. He argued that the Sandinistas were communists—a claim that had always brought American aid in the past.

But President Jimmy Carter had declared that human rights would be a key consideration in all foreign policy decisions. Any government that did not respect the basic rights of its citizens would receive little or no help from the United States. Somoza's government had done nothing to deserve arms or money, and there was no definite evidence that the Sandinistas were intending to establish a Marxist, pro-Soviet regime.

THE EARLY SANDINISTA REGIME

The Sandinistas inherited a country that was bankrupt and extensively damaged. During the war, the Somozas had transferred hundreds of millions of dollars to foreign banks. A mere $3.5 million remained in Nicaragua—a pittance compared to the country's total debts of $1,600 million, the largest per capita debt in all Latin America. A great deal of this debt had accumulated when General Somoza borrowed several million to buy arms to fight the revolutionaries. Now the victors had to pay those debts or lose all credit with the international banking and commercial community.

And never was the money needed more. So many factories and transportation facilities had been destroyed that over a third of the urban population had nowhere to work. Destruction was estimated at $2 billion. Furthermore, 70 percent of the farmland had not been sown, so food supplies were low and there were no agricultural products to export.

And who was to rebuild the country? Many of the upper-class people who had the technical, administrative, and financial skills needed to operate businesses, industries, and large farms had fled to other countries. Less than half the remaining population could read and write, and few of them had more than a basic education. The future did not look good, with malnourishment among children at about 65 percent. Establishing a stable government and rebuilding the country would not be easy under such conditions.

Members of the Sandinista government ride in triumph through the streets of Managua, Nicaragua, immediately after the overthrow of President Anastasio Somoza in July 1979.

The world kept a wary eye on the new Sandinista government. Would post-revolution Nicaragua repeat the precedent set by post-revolution Cuba? In Cuba the farms and industries had been nationalized and freedom severely restricted. Because of these radical policies, the Cuban economy was isolated from the world and had therefore never developed. Castro publicly advised the Sandinistas not to repeat his mistake. President Carter indirectly supported Castro's advice by indicating that Nicaragua would be eligible for U.S. economic aid only if it respected human rights, private property, and democratic principles.

The Sandinistas, now a political party rather than a guerrilla army, proceeded to create a mild and, under the circumstances, reasonable form of socialism. Most farms and industries remained private businesses that operated for profit in a free capitalistic economy. Banks were nationalized, but government ownership was the only option since they were bankrupt. Farms and industries owned by the Somozas, who had fled the country, were also nationalized.

Elections were scheduled for 1981. Until then a directorate of nine Sandinista leaders would decide government policy. A *junta* of five other Sandinistas would handle the day-to-day administration of the country. As a *junta*, these five would rule together (*junta* means "group" in Spanish) with no single member holding a higher office. The leaders promised to respect the freedom of the press and of religion, and the right of everyone to a fair trial, even former National Guard soldiers accused of war crimes.

Economic aid poured in from all over the world. President Carter, hoping to encourage the development of democracy and to maintain a friendly alliance, immediately put together a $75-million aid package, though it took Congress almost a year to certify that the Sandinistas were upholding democratic and capitalistic principles.

Meanwhile, Libya sent $100 million. Cuba, hoping to gain an ally on the mainland, sent 5,000 teachers, doctors, engineers, and military advisors. Other Soviet-bloc countries, including Vietnam, East Germany, and North Korea, sent trucks and military equipment. The U.S. State Department estimates that total military aid from the Soviet bloc exceeded $28 million in 1981.

DEMOCRACY DENIED

During its first two years, the new Nicaraguan government made no progress toward democracy. *La Prensa*, still owned and operated by the Chamorro family, was forced to shut down several times for opposing the government too vehemently. For a while the Archbishop of Nicaragua, Rivera y Damas, was prevented from speaking on the government television and radio stations, although he was allowed to continue operating the stations owned by the Catholic Church. Three business leaders who complained publicly that they could make no major business decisions without government approval were imprisoned for four months. When elections were postponed until 1985, two *junta* members who had strongly advocated the principles of private property, free enterprise, and democracy resigned in despair. One was Alfonso Robelo Callejas, a millionaire businessman who had backed the revolution. The other was Violeta Chamorro, widow of Joaquín Chamorro, the editor of *La Prensa* whose assassination had touched off the revolution. These *junta* members were never replaced, so the remaining *junta* was entirely in favor of a stronger form of socialism.

Another important defector from the Sandinista

ranks was Edén Pastora. Deciding that the revolution had simply replaced one dictatorship with another, he went into exile in Costa Rica and was soon joined by Alfonso Robelo and other political moderates who were dissatisfied with what they had helped to create.

After the defection of Alfonso Robelo, the most prominent member of the *junta* was its coordinator, Daniel Ortega Saavedra, who also served on the directorate that created national policies. Since his brother, Humberto Ortega, was Minister of Defense, Daniel was assumed to hold the most power in the government.

Despite its economic problems, Nicaragua began a rapid build-up of military strength. Cuban advisors helped train an army of 30,000 that was equipped with modern Soviet automatic rifles, tanks, and helicopters, and trucks and troop carriers from East Germany. Airport runways were extended in order to handle Russian MIG fighter jets, and pilots were sent to Eastern Europe for training. A civilian militia of 70,000, organized and trained by Edén Pastora before he left the country, was ready to protect local neighborhoods and factories. Within two years Nicaragua had the largest, most powerful armed forces in Central America.

The Nicaraguans claimed that they were building up their army in fear of invasion by former National Guard soldiers. This fear was not unfounded. There were several clashes between the Nicaraguan militia and ex-Somocista forces along the Honduran border. Meanwhile, some 600 Nicaraguan and Cuban exiles were undergoing military training at a private camp in Florida. Accused of preparing an invasion force, the White House denied any connection with the camp and said that since the camp was on private property there was nothing illegal about it. The intentions of the trainees were a secret, but Nicaragua assumed the worst. By 1983, that assumption would prove true.

DOMINOES OR SEPARATE SITUATIONS?

Revolutionary activity was not confined to Nicaragua in the late 1970s and early 1980s. El Salvador and Guatemala were both suffering civil wars that appeared to be similar to Nicaragua's. These wars had begun slowly a decade earlier but had intensified after the Sandinista victory in 1979. The connection between Nicaragua's successful revolution and increased leftist guerrilla activity elsewhere was too probable to ignore. When Ronald Reagan became president in January 1981 and appointed Alexander Haig Secretary of State, U.S. foreign policy in Latin America changed substantially from that of President Carter's administration.

Critics of President Carter say that he practically handed Nicaragua to the Cubans by not supporting Somoza. They maintain that if Carter had continued in office, he probably would have let the rightist governments of El Salvador and Guatemala fall, too, because of their extreme abuses of human rights.

President Reagan, Secretary Haig, and a large part of the Congress and Senate saw the Central American situation not as an instance of impoverished people rebelling against tyranny but rather as a case of Soviet-backed communist influence creeping north toward the U.S. border. They cited the domino theory, claiming that Cuba was the first domino and Nicaragua the second. In Secretary Haig's words, Nicaragua had become "a base for the export of subversion and armed intervention." Haig saw this development as a Soviet military campaign aimed, ultimately, at an attack against the United States.

Opponents of this idea felt that the causes of the rebellions in Central America were deeply rooted in the region's history. All the troubled nations had dictatorships, small wealthy classes, and huge impoverished classes. Such conditions made any country vulnerable to revolt. They argued that even if these countries were completely cut off from Nicaragua, their revolutions would continue.

But in February 1981, the U.S. State Department offered proof that clandestine Soviet and Cuban military support was flowing through Nicaragua into El Salvador. The report, entitled "Communist Influence in El Salvador," was based on captured guerrilla documents and war materials.

The documents described shipments coming from Nicaragua. Captured weapons, although made in several countries, were traced to the Soviet bloc. Vietnam, for example, apparently had sent American M-16s captured during the war there. There were also reports of weapons found in light planes that crashed in El Salvador after crossing the border from Nicaragua.

The Reagan administration intended to use this report as justification for supporting the government of El Salvador and possibly for taking military action against Nicaragua. But the *Wall Street Journal* and the *Washington Post* examined the evidence and found many problems. Many facts were wrong and the translation of the captured documents was poor. In one case, the State Department report cited shipments from Cuba to Nicaragua while the original document from the guerrillas said the shipment had gone in the other direction.

These criticisms did not change the conclusions of the report, but the State Department lost a good deal of credibility. After that, the American public and the Congress and Senate were less inclined to believe the

Reagan administration's warnings that Cuba and Nicaragua were united in a plot to take over Central America.

THE WELL-KNOWN SECRET WAR

In March 1982, the Nicaraguan government declared a state of emergency and placed its security forces on full alert because two bridges had been blown up near the Honduran border. After several smaller incidents occurred during the year, Nicaragua claimed that this was the beginning of a long-expected invasion by CIA-supported counterrevolutionaries. The White House said it was U.S. policy to neither confirm nor deny such accusations but commented that "the United States is not in the habit of engaging in sinister plots." The Nicaraguan state of emergency, meanwhile, meant the curtailment of several constitutional rights. Newspapers were put under censorship, and prominent opponents of the government were forbidden to leave the country.

There were also reports that the Sandinistas were persecuting the Miskito Indians who lived near the Honduran border. These isolated and fiercely independent people, who make up about 4 percent of the Nicaraguan population, were neither for nor against the revolution. But the Sandinistas tended to assume that whoever was not for the revolution was against it. To prevent the Miskitos from siding with the counterrevolutionaries in Honduras, the Nicaraguan military was forcibly moving the entire Miskito population to other locations. The relocation was not peaceful, however. A former official of the Sandinista intelligence agency who defected to the United States reported that hundreds of Indians were being methodically slaughtered.

Secretary of State Haig said that the curtailment of

human rights and the persecution of the Miskito Indians were proof that Nicaragua had no intentions of becoming a democracy. This, he said, was all the more reason to attempt to overthrow the Sandinistas.

By the end of 1982, it was no secret that as many as 5,000 counterrevolutionaries, who became known as *contras* (which means "counter" or "against" in Spanish), had infiltrated Nicaragua from Honduras. It was also no secret that this army, which called itself the Nicaraguan Democratic Front (FDN) had been covertly trained, supplied, and organized by the CIA.

Although the CIA backing was referred to as "covert" aid, the only secret about the support of the *contras* was the exact amount of money involved. CIA officials reported to Congress that the rebels' mission was to intercept Nicaraguan arms shipments to Salvadoran rebels. But as *contra* operations expanded and journalists began to interview *contras* on television, it became apparent to everyone that the *contras* were intending to overthrow, or at least harass, the Sandinistas. When *contra* planes, supplied by the CIA, began bombing missions against Nicaraguan airports and fuel depots, their alleged purpose was doubted even more.

The Democrats, who held the majority in the House of Representatives, did not like the idea of using the *contras* to conquer Nicaragua. Representatives pointed out that the invasion made the United States look imperialistic, was further destabilizing the region, and was not likely to end in victory. In an attempt to cut off the covert aid, Congress passed the Boland Amendment in December 1982. Named after its chief sponsor, Massachusetts Democrat Edward Boland, the bill specifically prohibited funds for forces trying to overthrow the government of Nicaragua.

The Boland Amendment had no effect, however,

**Former Sandinista leader Edén Pastora
(center) is shown here with members
of his *contra* army who are fighting to
overthrow the revolutionary government.**

because the Reagan administration maintained that the *contras* were not trying to overthrow the Sandinistas. Six months later, Congress passed a similar bill that specifically cut off covert aid to the *contras* but appropriated $80 million for overt aid to any Latin American country that would help patrol the borders of El Salvador in order to stop arms shipments. This bill was little more than a gesture of intent. Congress knew that the Senate, whose Republican majority tended to support the President's programs, would probably not pass the bill. And if the bill did survive to reach the President's desk, he would veto it.

ANOTHER CONTRA ARMY

Just as the FDN invasion was gaining force in the north near the Honduran border, another counter-revolutionary group, called the Democratic Revolutionary Alliance (ARDE), was attacking in the south, near Costa Rica. The leaders of this rebel force were the two former Sandinistas: Edén Pastora Gomez and Alfonso Robelo Callejas.

In talks with U.S. Representatives and journalists, Pastora and Robelo explained that they intended to fulfill the original purpose of the Sandinista revolution—the creation of a true democracy in Nicaragua. The Alliance disavowed any connection with the FDN, claiming that many members of that army were former soldiers of Somoza's National Guard who wanted to establish another rightist regime. The Alliance did, however, accept a small amount of covert support from the CIA.

Although smaller in numbers and weaker in arms, the Alliance eventually may cause the Sandinistas more problems than the FDN. Edén Pastora is still a popular figure in Nicaragua. If general disenchantment with the Sandinistas grows, the people's support may swing to the *contras* of the Alliance rather than those of the FDN. During the first three months of the Alliance campaign, their ranks swelled from 500 to 2,000 members but they were making little progress from the uninhabited swamps hear the Costa Rican border.

A PAPAL VISIT

Pope John Paul II made an eight-day trip through Nicaragua, Panama, El Salvador, Guatemala, Honduras, Belize, and Haiti in March 1983. It was the first time in modern history that a Pope had visited an area torn by war. Explaining why he came, the Pope said, "One should be with those who suffer." Those who were suffering in this case were a flock of nearly 25 million Roman Catholics; 100,000 had already died in the long struggle between left and right.

Pope John Paul II brought more than hope and solace, however. He had harsh words for liberal-minded Catholics in Nicaragua, El Salvador, and Guatemala. In these countries some church leaders were taking the Theology of Liberation to extremes, advocating violent rebellion and forging a new church that included Marxism among its beliefs.

Two priests in particular concerned the Pope. They were Nicaraguan Foreign Minister Miguel d'Escoto Brockman, and Minister of Culture Ernesto Cardenal Martinez. John Paul wanted both to resign from the government. Miguel d'Escoto was conveniently out of the country during the papal visit, but Martinez had to face the irate Pontiff. Arriving at the airport in a white shirt, blue work pants, and a black beret, the errant priest was denied the right to kiss the Pope's ring. John Paul told him, "You must straighten out your position with the church."

On his arrival in Managua,
Pope John Paul II listens as
Daniel Ortega, coordinator of the
Sandinista junta, gives a speech
denouncing U.S. policy in Central America.

Many people thought John Paul's reception in Nicaragua was not worthy of a pope. At the airport in Managua, the Pontiff had to stand in the sun for twenty-five minutes while Daniel Ortega Saavedra gave a speech glorifying the revolution and denouncing U.S. imperialism. At an outdoor mass for 500,000 people, neither the government nor the local church had bothered to erect a cross. During John Paul's sermon, youths interrupted him several times, chanting, "Power to the people!" and "We want peace!" He responded by angrily shouting, "Silence! The Church is the first in favor of peace!"

OFFICIALS OUSTED, CONSULATES CLOSED

Soon after the Pope's visit, on June 6, 1983, Nicaragua announced it was deporting three American diplomats accused of espionage and covert subversion. One was accused of plotting to poison the Nicaraguan Foreign Minister Miguel d'Escoto. The U.S. State Department denied the charges, calling them ludicrous lies. In retaliation for the expulsion, the State Department ordered the closing of the six Nicaraguan consulates in the United States. The six diplomats in charge of those offices were given twenty-four hours to leave the country. Fifteen other officials were given four days.

The back-to-back expulsions fell short of severing diplomatic relations between Nicaragua and the United States. Embassies in both countries continued to operate, and a visit to Managua later that week by the United States special envoy to Central America Richard Stone was held as scheduled. Richard Stone had been given a difficult assignment by President Reagan—to find a solution to the problems in Central America. His first visit to Nicaragua was not an optimistic start. During a twenty-four-hour meeting with Daniel Ortega and Miguel d'Escoto, Stone heard complaints about the U.S.-backed *contras*. He replied by suggesting that the invasion could be stopped if Nicaragua reduced the number of Cuban advisors in the country, halted shipments of arms to Salvadoran guerrillas, and negotiated with the invading *contras* about participation in Nicaraguan politics. Stone left without reaching any agreements, but within a month Daniel Ortega offered a peace proposal. He suggested regional negotiations involving all the countries of Central America, a freeze on arms shipments to both sides of the civil war in El Salvador, and a ban on all foreign military bases and training in Central America. This would apply to both the United States and Cuba.

President Reagan expressed interest in the proposal but raised the question of how to verify Nicaragua's adherence to any agreements. There was no other U.S. response to Nicaragua's offer before the following week, when some startling events changed the situation. President Reagan ordered extensive U.S. military maneuvers in the area. Designated "operation Big Pine II," the maneuvers called for two aircraft carriers, a battleship, and accompanying fleets—a total of nineteen warships—to patrol in international waters off the Pacific and Caribbean coasts of Nicaragua. Meanwhile, 5,000 American troops would stage training maneuvers in Honduras, and army engineers there would clear runways for transport and fighter planes.

While President Reagan's stated purpose for the maneuvers was to train U.S. forces, Nicaraguans, Cubans, and many Americans saw it as a show of force and perhaps an overture to war. The United States had staged war games in the region before, but never had fleets been stationed off the coast of a specific country as a kind of silent threat. In a Washington press conference, President Reagan was asked repeatedly whether he was planning to invade or set up a blockade around Nicaragua. His answer was negative, but the Sandinistas were not convinced. Already battling contra guerrillas inside their borders, they now faced war fleets as well as a nearby build-up of land forces.

The announcement of Big Pine II came amid rumors of other military build-ups. An unidentified White House official intimated to reporters that the president was considering expanding covert operations in Central America and was hoping to increase the number of U.S. military advisors in El Salvador from 55 to 125. Meanwhile, the CIA reported that Soviet shipments of military equipment had doubled since 1982 but that most of the equipment was of a defensive nature. This contradicted President Reagan's claim that Nicaragua was a threat to the rest of Central America. The CIA also reported that Nicaraguan arms shipments to rebels in El Salvador had been negligible for several months.

All this information came during the week when Congress was debating whether to cut off covert aid to the contras. The vote was close—228 against the measure and 195 in favor of it. Many representatives admitted confusion and nervous concern about the sudden events. By all appearances, the administration was pushing toward a military solution to Central America's problems. One member of Congress called it a risky "quick fix" that might make President Reagan look good in the next year's elections but would not really solve any of the deep-rooted, long-term problems of the area. The members of Congress were also concerned about those elections. None of them wanted to be accused of "losing" Central America to a communist takeover.

President Reagan had one point that was hard to deny. No peaceful solutions were possible in Central America if leftist guerrillas continued to destroy anything that was built. Fertilizer, schoolbooks, and elections could not defeat bombs and bullets. Before any country could solve its social and economic problems, it had to have the peace that makes long-term solutions possible. And if both sides refused to negotiate, peace would be possible only through military victory.

The pressures put on Nicaragua were actually aimed at relieving pressure in El Salvador. The Reagan administration argued that the Sandinistas would stop the flow of supplies to El Salvador if Nicaragua were threatened with attack. Secretary of State George Shultz called this a strategy of "symmetry" in which Nicaraguan aid to rebels in El Salvador was balanced by U.S. aid to rebels in Nicaragua. One White House official put it more simply, saying that the United States was just "exchanging one dirty little war for another."

The Reagan administration declared that it had "drawn the line" in El Salvador. Nicaragua might have been lost to Soviet influence, but communism would not be allowed to creep farther. To prevent a communist takeover in El Salvador, the United States has been promoting social, political, and economic reform while supporting the Salvadoran military in its civil war against guerrillas. There have been successes and failures, and the situation has similarities to and differences from that of Nicaragua before the fall of Somoza. Whether El Salvador will follow the example of Nicaragua or is successfully searching for better solutions is a question worth investigating.

EL SALVADOR

During a period at the end of the nineteenth century and the beginning of the twentieth, El Salvador converted from an economy based on subsistence crops to one based on cash crops. Instead of growing beans and corn on small farms to feed the people who actually worked the land, El Salvador began growing coffee on large plantations to export in exchange for cash.

This system was fine for people who owned the coffee plantations and those who still had land on which to grow their own food. But gradually the coffee farmers became wealthy while subsistence farmers had nothing but food. Consequently, the landowners always had money with which to buy more land, while the poorer farmers always had to sell land in order to have money to buy seed and fertilizer or to pay their debts. Over the years, the coffee growers amassed great wealth and vast plantations as hundreds of thousands of poor people became landless farmers who were forced, by law, to accept low-paying jobs on plantations.

THE REBELLION OF 1932

The Great Depression of the 1930s hit El Salvador especially hard. With the world economy at a standstill and millions of people out of work, few had money for the luxury of coffee. Prices plummeted, and El Salvador faced two problems: it had nowhere to sell its cash crops, and it had little land for subsistence crops. There was little money or food except for the few people in the rich upper class. The majority of the Salvadorans had nothing to lose, so they were quite willing to try anything new.

In 1930, a young Salvadoran named Agustín Farabundo Marti arrived from Nicaragua where he had been fighting alongside Augusto Sandino. Marti founded the Salvadoran Communist Party and told the peasants of his country that a communist revolution by the lower class would bring about economic equality and social justice. Everyone would have land, he said. No one would be forced by law to work on someone else's farm, and those who had no jobs would be fed, not arrested.

The peasants, mostly illiterate Indians, understood nothing about communism, but they liked its promises. They were not soldiers, however, so when they raised their machetes and pitchforks in revolt, they killed fewer than 100 people before the Salvadoran army crushed their rebellion. Then, to completely wipe out the idea of communism, the army proceeded to kill anyone who looked like an Indian. Between 15,000 and 30,000 unarmed civilians were exterminated, more than ten times the number that probably participated in the rebellion. The exact figures are not known because all government records from that period have disappeared.

Since the rebellion, the upper class has controlled the military and the military has controlled the government. Until 1982, military officers ruled the country as dictators. They were expected to cooperate with business leaders and large landowners by passing and enforcing laws that preserved the social and economic structure. For example, labor unions were not allowed to grow strong because they would help the lower class and threaten the wealth of the upper class. Any president who "leaned to the left" by letting workers go on strike or by allowing the socialist or communist party to participate in an election would lose financial support. The upper class would simply hire other officers to carry out a military coup. The president would be forced out of office and someone else would establish an administration more cooperative with the landowners and upper-class business people.

THE SALVADORANS

Today there are about 5 million Salvadorans living in an area the size of Massachusetts, making El Salvador the most crowded mainland country in the western hemisphere. For a primarily agricultural country, this situation is disastrous. Although industry developed substantially in the 1960s, the number of factory jobs did not increase as fast as the population. Agriculture remains the principal business in El Salvador, but by 1980, just 2 percent of the population owned half of all the farmland.

The poverty is appalling. Three-quarters of Salvadoran children are malnourished. Forty-five percent of all deaths occur in childhood. Less than half the surviving children learn to read and write, and far fewer reach the sixth grade.

Over half the population are migrant workers known as *jornaleros*. They have no homes and no land. During planting and harvest seasons, they can earn wages on coffee, sugar, and cotton plantations. But they can earn only $5.70 a day, which leaves little to save. If a worker does not like the offered wage, the landowner has hundreds of starving people outside the farm gate who would gladly take the job.

During the rainy season, from May to October, the *jornaleros* have no work. They camp along the roads, living under packing crates or cardboard lean-tos. Respiratory and intestinal ailments kill them by the thousands. No medical care is available outside the cities.

In short, the lower class in El Salvador has little or no hope. Those who still own or rent a piece of land are bound to lose it. Those without land can expect to be hungry until they die. Parents know that half their children will die young and the other half will live in misery. Like the rebels of 1932, these people have little to live for and nothing to lose by fighting for any kind of change.

The wealth of the upper class and the poverty of the lower class have been perpetuated by the force of the government and the military. The constitution of El Salvador lists such rights as freedom of religion and the press and the right to elections and fair trials, but it has been generally ignored. Elections have almost all been fraudulent, police have arrested and executed tens of thousands of people without court order or trial, death squads have been allowed to operate freely, political parties have been harassed, churches have been bombed and church workers, murdered.

The government and upper class claim that the victims of these crimes are "subversives" who are trying to undermine the government of El Salvador. Actually, they are often people who have done no more than complain about injustice, talk about labor unions or strikes, or advocate a change in the political and social structure of El Salvador. To keep an eye on suspected subversives, the government formed a paramilitary organization called ORDEN. ORDEN was a network of civilians who, in hopes of receiving rewards or favors, acted as spies in every town, village, and farm. When they reported secret meetings, talks of labor strikes, or sermons that criticized the government, the people involved often "disappeared" and were later found dead beside the road, in a garbage dump, or at the bottom of a cliff.

Most indicative of government disrespect for the lower class have been attacks against the Church. In 1980 alone, several church workers and eleven clergy members were murdered. One of them was Archbishop of El Salvador, Oscar Arnulfo Romero, who was gunned down while saying mass on March 23, 1980. Although he was the most widely loved and respected man in the country, he had been branded a leftist subversive for organizing the Legal Aid Commission that kept track of murdered civilians and those who "disappeared," for preaching that God did not want anyone to live in poverty, and finally for asking all soldiers to disobey the orders of their officers because a higher authority said, "Thou shalt not kill." Not surprisingly, Romero's assassin was never caught.

A DECADE OF UNREST

During the 1970s, the situation in El Salvador became worse. Small guerrilla bands in the mountains grew larger and bolder. Secret political action organizations organized mass demonstrations that drew as many as 100,000 people to the streets of San Salvador. Some of these guerrillas and organizers were hard-core communists, but most were people who were simply angry at the government and the upper class that mistreated the great masses of poor people.

In the 1972 presidential election, the mayor of San Salvador, José Napoleón Duarte, was allowed to run for president. As a member of the Christian Democrat party, he was a political moderate who wanted a constitutionally legal government and more help for the poor. But when he began to gain more votes than the military's candidate, he was arrested, tortured, and sent into exile. Another general became president, and government repression of political activities increased. In response, guerrilla activity also increased. Many wealthy people were kidnapped and held for ransom. Several foreign embassies were taken over and some factories were burned down.

In October 1979, two army colonels marched into the office of the president, Carlos Humberto Romero, and announced that they were taking over the government. When President Romero found out that they had the support of many other officers, he fled to Guatemala, never to return.

The American ambassador to El Salvador, Frank Devine, suspected that the colonels were reacting to events in Nicaragua, where the Sandinistas had just overthrown the Somoza regime after Somoza's unsuccessful fight to the finish. The colonels probably thought that the same would happen in El Salvador if nothing was done.

The two colonels announced that they would join in a *junta* with three civilians and would begin a sweeping social reform. They promised to release all political prisoners and to stop the death squads that kidnapped and killed supposed subversives. The armed forces, which so often killed innocent civilians in their ruthless hunt for guerrillas, would be brought under control. ORDEN would be dissolved. And most significantly, they promised a land reform program in which the farms of upper-class landowners would be broken up and distributed among poor peasants.

Archbishop Romero asked the people of El Salvador to be patient with their new government. But its promises were never fufilled. Few prisoners were released, and those who had "disappeared" in the prisons were not found, nor was their absence explained. The land reform program never developed, and the military was by no means more careful to avoid attacks on civilians. On October 24, 1979, during a peaceful mass demonstration in San Salvador, soldiers in a truck fired machine guns into a crowd on the steps of a cathedral, killing twenty-four. News cameras caught the action, and the whole world saw the slaughter. When the *junta* tried to investigate, José García, minister of defense, made it clear that he alone controlled all military matters. No investigation was carried out.

One by one, civilian *junta* members resigned and were replaced as they learned that the colonels were not sharing the power and that José García would take orders from no one. By March 1980, no qualified civilians were willing to serve in the *junta*. The United States threatened to cut off all foreign aid if the government had no civilian participation.

Aware that it could not survive without U.S. backing, the *junta* announced a program of land reform, the Agrarian Transformation Act, on March 6, 1980. This land reform promised to turn over a great deal of land to landless peasants. The next day the *junta* announced that the government was nationalizing all banks and export companies in order to provide full support for the new peasant farms. These were the two most important days in El Salvador since 1932, and on March 9, José Duarte, who had returned from exile in Venezuela, agreed to serve as civilian president of the junta.

THE LAND REFORM

The United States and U.S. Ambassador Robert E. White strongly supported the idea of land reform. It was felt that if the Salvadoran government offered the peasants the land they wanted, and if the economic strength of the upper class were weakened, no one would have reason to support the guerrillas.

The Agrarian Transformation Act planned the most extensive land redistribution plan ever carried out without a communist revolution. It was to come about in three phases.

Phase I, effective immediately, expropriated all farms of 1250 acres (500 ha) or more. Most of these were the huge cotton and sugar cane plantations in low-lying areas, and the cattle farms of the interior mountainous areas. Peasant workers currently living on these farms would be able to buy small separate plots while sharing such resources as tractors, trucks, and other machinery as communal property.

Phase II, to take place at an unspecified time in the future, would redistribute the medium-sized farms of 250 to 1,250 acres. This was the most important land— coffee farms with the cash crop that was the base of upper-class wealth.

Phase III, called the "land-to-the-tiller" program, would turn over small plots of land to whoever was renting, sharecropping, or otherwise farming but not owning the land they lived on.

LAND REFORM PROBLEMS

The plan was far from perfect. The land affected by Phase I was the poorest in El Salvador; over two-thirds of it was unsuitable for cash crops. And the landowners used every available loophole to minimize their losses. Since the plan allowed them to keep as much as 450 acres, they naturally turned over the worst acreage to the peasants. They first removed all cattle, seed, fertilizer, irrigation systems, tools, and even barbed-wire fences. The new peasant landowners had to start with nothing, which made profit a very distant, if not impossible, goal.

The *junta* assigned the Ministry of Defense the duty of enforcing the land reform program. Many people felt this was a case of putting the fox in charge of the chickens. The military, they said, was still under the control of the upper class. And there were innumerable instances of death squads with army weapons and jeeps. It was obvious they had the cooperation of the army and National Guard as they easily evaded army roadblocks to drive onto the communal peasant farms. There they arrested commune leaders and left them dead—and often mutilated—not far from the farms. José Duarte, president of the *junta*, admitted regretfully that a soldier could be hired for death squad duty for $40 a month plus a life insurance policy. Duarte claimed to know of one landowner who had invested $2 million dollars in death squad activities.

During 1980, over 200 farm leaders were murdered, but Salvadorans were not the only victims of rightist, antireform workers. Two American land reform experts, Mark Pearlman and Mike Hammer, were gunned down as they ate dinner in a San Salvador hotel. They had been sent by the American labor organization, the AFL-CIO, to help organize the land reform and the new communal farms. The assassin later confessed and revealed the name of the officer who ordered him to murder the two men. The officer was never brought to trial.

The leftist guerrilla army also worked against the reform program. It, too, wanted the farms to fail because if the program satisfied too many people, too few would support the rebellion. Guerrilla activities were not murderous like those of the rightist death squads, but guerrillas burned trucks full of crops, destroyed bridges between the farms and the market, cut the power lines that supplied the farms with electricity, and in some cases shot at people in fields to scare them away from their work.

Despite these many problems, the governments of El Salvador and the United States considered the land reform a political success. Although it by no means stopped all support for the guerrillas, it apparently helped prevent a massive general uprising like the one that had overthrown the Somoza regime in Nicaragua. In January 1981, when the clandestine guerrilla radio station, called *Venceremos*, announced a final offensive and called for all Salvadorans to take up arms against their oppressors, no such popular support appeared. The offensive was beaten back easily. The *junta* proudly claimed that the lower class now had an interest in the survival of its government. Hundreds of thousands of people had either land or a promise of it and so had nothing to gain from a leftist takeover.

But shortly after the offensive, the *junta* announced that the land reform would cease until the country was politically stable. Phase I was substantially complete, although most peasants still had not received title to their land. Over the next few years, about 8 percent per year were evicted from their new holdings. Phase III had just barely begun, and Phase II, the most important because it had involved the coffee land, would not even be started. According to opponents of the government, this was proof that the situation in El Salvador had not changed; the upper class was still in control. As a kind of insurance policy, they had given up their worst acreage in order to preserve their valuable coffee land, the basis of their wealth.

LEFTIST STRATEGY

Small guerrilla bands have been operating in El Salvador since the 1932 rebellion. During the 1970s,

**Salvadoran guerrillas show off
their battle flag in a village
they captured the day before.**

these bands built up into small armies, and in 1980, the various groups united to form the Farabundo Marti National Liberation Front (FMLN). Currently, the FMLN is estimated to have about 5,000 armed members. The greater part of the FMLN are the *jornaleros*, the migrant workers who gained nothing from the land reform program. Although generally termed "leftists," many of them know nothing about communism or socialism. They are simply angry at the upper class that keeps them poor, and at the government and military that have quite likely killed at least one family member or friend.

The FMLN strategy is very hard to combat. Its attacks have not been against the military as much as against the economy. By burning factories, blowing up bridges, downing powerlines, and destroying trucks and buses, FMLN members are trying to drive El Salvador into economic chaos. That, they hope, will make all Salvadorans rise up against the government.

The guerrillas have been careful not to attack civilians directly. In fact, in the areas they control, they set up hospitals and schools. A guerrilla camp often looks like a small village complete with fields, farm animals, and entire families.

For the FMLN, a military stalemate is a victory. The objective to slowly wear down the government. When its members take over a town, they usually stay only until the army or National Guard arrives. The armed forces are not large enough to protect all towns, and they lack the air force mobility needed to conduct large-scale operations in the jungles and mountains far from the cities. So when they leave an area, the guerrillas quickly take control again.

While the guerrillas are the military arm of the rebellion, the Democratic Revolution Front (FDR) is its political organization. The FDR is a union of all leftist political parties in El Salvador. Currently, Guillermo Ungo, who ran as José Duarte's vice presidential candidate during the disastrous elections of 1972, is the leader of the FDR. During many trips to the United States and Europe, Mr. Ungo has said that the FDR wants to negotiate an end to the civil war. He also claims that the FDR wants to establish a democratic government in El Salvador and that his party is not aligned with Cuba or the Soviet Union. However, many people question whether the guerrillas would accept any settlement negotiated by the FDR.

THE MILITARY'S RESPONSE

The military is having a difficult time just maintaining a stalemate. Since guerrillas do not wear uniforms and since their supporters can be virtually anyone, the military has too often attacked innocent and unarmed citizens. The Legal Aid Commission of the Catholic Church in El Salvador reports that of the 37,000 killed in the war, by 1983 over 90 percent were unarmed. Some of the killing was by mistake, but some is due to a terrible tendency to kill anyone who was remotely suspect. Often soldiers have been horribly cruel simply to terrorize civilians into avoiding all contact with the guerrillas. The Legal Aid Commission and Amnesty International have records of extensive cases of mass murder, infanticide, rape, torture, and mutilation. In a few cases, entire villages were slaughtered. In one case, the Air Force leveled a town that had been evacuated by the guerrillas just a few hours before.

In 1981, when 1,500 Salvadoran soldiers came to the United States for training in antiguerrilla warfare, one essential lesson was the importance of respecting the civilian population. The training had some effect, but it did not entirely solve the problem. Civilian deaths dropped, at least temporarily, from about 300 to 100 a week—an improvement, but hardly perfection.

The military has been criticized for lacking any effective strategy. With large units based in the capital cities of each *departamento*, the garrisons in the villages are so small that they are easily overrun by guerrillas. The military's response is to send a convoy of troops to retake the town. Their arrival is predictable, however, so the guerrillas often have an ambush and a timely, temporary retreat prepared. The army regains control easily enough, but only until the unit returns to its base.

INCREASING U. S. INVOLVEMENT

In December 1980, the deaths of four American church people awoke the concern of many Americans. The dead were three nuns—Maura Clark, Dorothy Kazel, and Ita Ford—and a lay worker, Jean Donovan. They had been followed from the San Salvador airport by soldiers and were later found buried in a shallow grave near the road. All had been shot and two showed evidence of rape. Ironically, the bullets that killed them were made in the United States. The incident would affect U.S. policy for several years as Americans seriously questioned whether the government of El Salvador was worth supporting.

President Carter cut off all U.S. aid until El Salvador carried out an investigation of the murders. But when the guerrillas launched their January 1981 offensive, just prior to Ronald Reagan's inauguration, Carter reluctantly sent $10 million in emergency military aid and approved the idea of sending a small number of military advisors to train Salvadoran troops.

The Reagan administration took a stronger stance against the revolutionaries in El Salvador and against the Sandinistas in Nicaragua. In February, President

Reagan first dropped the insistence on an investigation of the murders of the American church women as a requirement for U.S. aid. Later that month the State Department, under the control of Secretary Alexander Haig, issued a white-paper report, "Communist Interference in El Salvador." The brief report, as discussed in the chapter on Nicaragua, gave evidence of Nicaraguan, Cuban, and probably Soviet cooperation in the supplying of arms to Salvadoran guerrillas. A few days after the report was issued, $25 million in military aid and fifty-six military advisors were sent to El Salvador.

ANOTHER VIETNAM?

To many people, the situation looked very much like the beginning of the war in Vietnam. There, twenty years earlier, a war against communist guerrillas had involved ever-increasing amounts of U.S. military assistance. A decade of fighting, billions of dollars in weapons and training, and the deaths of over 50,000 American soldiers ended in United States withdrawal and a communist takeover.

Could El Salvador become another Vietnam? There are many similarities between the two situations and the U.S. policies pursued in the early stages of the two conflicts. Both El Salvador and Vietnam had large, illiterate lower classes and powerful, elite upper classes. Both countries were good territories for guerrillas—heavily forested and without good transportation routes. The armies of both were poorly trained and

A United States adviser teaches a Salvadoran air force cadet how to use a mortar.

led by officers not very dedicated to defeating the enemy. Their governments, always afraid of a military coup, selected officers for their loyalty, not their capabilities.

U.S. involvement in Vietnam began slowly, with a few advisors. Claiming that the fighting was directly caused by Soviet and Chinese strategies of international aggression, President Lyndon B. Johnson easily found the congressional backing necessary to send greater numbers of advisors and, eventually, combat troops.

The situation in El Salvador is very similar, but there are also key differences. Human rights are of more concern now than then, and Americans more readily question the moral quality of the foreign governments that the United States supports. Perhaps the most important difference may be the memory of the war in Vietnam. Many Americans see it as a hard-earned lesson, a mistake that could not be excused a second time. When in 1981 the first advisors went to El Salvador, 20,000 protestors demonstrated in Washington, D.C. It was the largest demonstration since the war in Vietnam, and it cautioned the government against becoming entangled in another overseas battle against guerrillas on their own territory. Congress reacted by passing a bill that required the president to certify, twice a year, that the Salvadoran government and military forces were improving the human rights situation and were preparing to negotiate with the leftists.

FREE ELECTIONS

In March 1982, El Salvador held elections for a parliamentary assembly. This assembly was to draft a constitution and prepare the country for a presidential election.

The FDR and the guerrillas refused to participate in

the elections. FDR leader Guillermo Ungo claimed, quite reasonably, that any leftist who dared campaign would be committing suicide. According to the leftists, this made the elections invalid.

Despite guerrilla threats against anyone who voted, the people of El Salvador turned out in overwhelming numbers. An estimated 80 percent of the adult population cast votes. Observers from the United States and several other countries verified that the election was conducted honestly.

The results surprised many. The moderate Christian Democrat party led by José Duarte gained more assembly seats than any other single party, but the combined seats of all the rightist parties made up the greatest total.

The assembly elected Roberto D'Abuisson, a vehement antileftist, as its president. (The position of president of the assembly was similar to that of the vice president of the United States.) Less than a year before, D'Abuisson had been arrested for plotting to overthrow the civilian/military *junta*. Ambassador Robert E. White had called him a "pathological killer," and many people are sure D'Abuisson hired the assassin of Archbishop Oscar Romero.

The assembly elected Christian Democrat Alvaro Magaña to serve as provisional president of El Salvador. Magaña has kept a low profile, working with the assembly to formulate a constitution but doing little to further the land reform or bring the armed forces under control. Since rightists held the majority of assembly seats, and since no elected official controlled the armed forces, there was little Magaña could do to bring about change.

THE REAGAN-DODD DEBATE

President Reagan called a joint session of the Congress and the Senate in April 1983 so he could explain the

At inauguration ceremonies for El Salvador's
newly elected government, assembly president,
Roberto D'Abuisson, is flanked by provisional
president, Alvaro Magaña (right), and
outgoing president, José Napoleón Duarte (left).

importance of military and economic support for the Salvadoran government. He also wanted to justify continued support of the anti-Sandinista rebels who had invaded Nicaragua. The principal points of the president's speech and the rebuttal given by Democratic Senator Christopher Dodd of Connecticut bring up the most important questions about El Salvador.

President Reagan stressed that Central America is strategically important because it is so close to the United States and to the shipping lanes of the Caribbean Sea and the Panama Canal. He claimed that human rights progress had been made in El Salvador, that the land reform had given land to almost half a million peasants, and that the elections had given El Salvador its first democratically elected government in fifty years. It would not be right, he said, to let leftist guerrillas overthrow that government just because they had better arms supplied by communist countries.

The president outlined four American goals in Central America:

- First, in response to the centuries of dictatorship and human rights abuses, the United States would support democracy, social reform, and liberty.
- Second, to meet the problems of the worldwide recession and, in El Salvador, the economic sabotage of the guerrillas, the United States would support economic development. In 1983, from every dollar in aid 77 cents would buy food, fertilizer, and other essentials of economic growth.
- Third, in response to the military challenge of Cuba and Nicaragua, U.S. military assistance, which would never include American combat troops, would be used to protect democratically elected governments.

- Fourth, the United States would support dialogues and negotiations both among the countries of Central America and between opposing forces within each country.

Concluding his speech, the president stated that the situation was critical. While the security of the United States was at stake, he said, the aid he was proposing to send to Central American countries, a total of $600 million in 1984, was less than a tenth of the amount Americans would spend on video games in that year.

Senator Christopher Dodd, speaking on behalf of the Democratic party after the president's speech, saw the Central American situation differently. He agreed that the United States should never allow another Marxist government in Central America and would never tolerate Soviet military bases or missiles there. But Senator Dodd went on to say that the president did not understand the causes of the conflict and therefore was not offering the right solutions.

The causes, said Dodd, were the rightist dictators, the widespread poverty, the death squads, the general injustice, and the hopeless plight of the majority of Central Americans. Under such conditions, rebellions are bound to erupt, with or without the help of Nicaragua or Cuba. And military solutions to such problems would fail just as they had failed in Vietnam.

According to Dodd, the solution had to be social, not military. The United States had to make violent revolution preventable by making peaceful revolution possible. The land reform would have to be carried out, the military and death squads would have to be controlled, and the government of El Salvador would have to negotiate with the leftists and find a way to have them participate in free elections.

Two weeks after the speeches, the Senate Foreign

Relations Committee approved an additional $20 million in military aid—one-third of what President Reagan had asked for. It was a compromise between the Republicans and the Democrats, created by dissatisfaction with the lack of alternatives. Many members of Congress, especially Democrats, felt that other nonmilitary efforts should be made. They thought that the administration could be doing more to promote free elections, negotiations with guerrillas, and broader policies that would encompass the common problems of the entire region.

To appease the legislative branch and narrow the gaps that divided them, President Reagan appointed ex-Senator Richard Stone special envoy to Central America in May 1983. As an ambassador-at-large, Stone was assigned the nearly impossible job of helping all Central American countries move toward democracy as they fought off insurgency. His first task was to help Salvadoran President Magaña include the leftists in the elections scheduled for February 1984. This goal would prove impossible, but it was politically important for President Reagan to show Congress—and for the United States to show the world—that nonmilitary alternatives were being pursued.

The leftists, however, did not see much opportunity in the invitation to join in the elections. They claimed it would be suicidal for them to run for office. Regardless of any promises made by the United States or El Salvador, leftists candidates would have been marked targets for death squads. Therefore, the FDR wanted a plan that would let its members assume positions in the government and the armed forces without being elected. Both President Reagan and President Magaña rejected this idea outright, however, explaining that no one should be allowed to "shoot their way into the government."

Within a few weeks of Stone's appointment, Secretary of State George Shultz announced that the ambassador to El Salvador, Deane Hinton, and the Assistant Secretary of State for Inter-American Affairs, Thomas O. Enders, were being replaced. Apparently both officials had been in some disagreement with President Reagan's policies. A few months earlier, Ambassador Hinton had said in a luncheon speech in San Salvador that the "gorillas" of the extreme right were as much a threat to El Salvador as the guerrillas of the extreme left. Thomas Enders had approved the speech beforehand. The implication that the guerrillas were not the sole cause of El Salvador's conflict had raised more questions in Congress and thus created more legislative difficulties for the president. The removal of the two officials indicated that the administration was intending to maintain one unified policy within its branch of the government.

Yet another shake-up in El Salvador was the replacement of the Minister of Defense José García, who had held that position since the coup of 1979. With the armed forces still locked in a stalemate with the guerrillas, García's strategies and competence were being questioned. A U.S. report said that the army was a "9-to-5, five-day-a-week" operation that tended to stay in the barracks after dark and on weekends. Although the soldiers were willing to take orders and fight, their officers seemed more concerned with personal advancement and the prestige of their rank. Meanwhile, the international press was branding the armed forces as unnecessarily cruel, and the upper class was complaining about the army's handling of the land reform program.

García was replaced by General Carlos Eugenio Vides Casanova, former director of the National Guard. General Vides launched a new strategy aimed at wiping out the guerrilla camps in a given area and then starting construction projects to repair roads, bridges, schools, and water systems. This strategy, which long beforehand had been suggested by U.S. military experts, was supposed to establish a better relationship between the armed forces and the *campesino* peasants. In its early stages, however, the plan was not very effective. As before, guerrillas would take control of the area as soon as the army left, and the construction projects would be destroyed. The problem was a shortage of troops, which prevented the military from securing several large areas simultaneously. The shortage was caused by a low reenlistment rate. Morale was very low, especially in battalions where officers were not dedicated and where troops were sometimes less well trained, armed, experienced, and motivated than the guerrillas they faced. Despite the change in leadership, the stalemate was not broken and the guerrillas continued to destroy the infrastructure of El Salvador. United States presidential candidate Walter Mondale commented that if the United States did not find a way to solve the problems of El Salvador, U.S. troops would inevitably have to be sent to uphold the government.

President Reagan, meanwhile, took a major step toward improving the quality of the Salvadoran army by approving the building and staffing of a training camp in Honduras. There U.S. advisors would be relatively safe and their presence would not appear to be a move toward "another Vietnam." It would also be less expensive and more efficient than sending Salvadoran troops to Fort Benning, Georgia, where 477 officer candidates had been trained in 1982. Some 2,400 troops were scheduled for training at the Honduran base. U.S. military personnel in Honduras, numbering 62 at the time, would triple to about 180. President Reagan was quick to point out that this number was miniscule compared to the estimated 2,000 to 3,000 Cuban military advisors in Nicaragua.

It was shortly after the announcement of the new base that President Reagan launched the Big Pine II military maneuvers in Honduras and off the coasts of Nicaragua. The two moves signaled to Nicaragua and Cuba that the United States was not going to abstain from all use of its military might. With Special Envoy Richard Stone now suggesting that he might meet with Salvadoran rebels, Cuba and Nicaragua saw that—given the choice—it would be wiser to have Salvadorans negotiate than to have the United States blockade their ports or even attack their territories. While publicly supporting the Salvadoran rebels, Managua and Havana were privately urging them to meet with the Americans. As one Sandinista put it, "We are practicing survival politics."

President Reagan's carrot-or-stick strategy showed early signs of working. In early 1983, envoy Stone met briefly in Bogotá, Colombia with Ruben Zamora, a leader of the FDR, the political arm of the leftist front. By no means a hard-line communist, Zamora had served on one of the civilian-military *juntas* that had tried to lead El Salvador just after the 1979 coup. In their ninety-minute talk, Stone tried to persuade the FDR to participate in the 1984 Salvadoran elections. Zamora reiterated that he did not believe the elections would be fair and that they would be too dangerous for leftist candidates. The two did not approach any agreement, except to meet again. Zamora termed the talks "a small step, but a step in the right direction. . . . If we can keep the flame of negotiations alive, this could be a deterrent to those in the Reagan administration who want to treat Central America as if they were in the nineteenth century."

THE DESPERATE EXPERIMENT

In many ways, the problem in El Salvador typifies a situation found throughout Latin America. For centuries, virtually every country south of the United

States was ruled by a rightest dictator who used military force to suppress the poor, enrich the wealthy, and preserve the power of the leaders. In many countries, this scenario continues into the 1980s. In most others, democracies are so shaky that a military coup could, at any moment, throw the country back into the political system of the last century. And virtually every country has guerrilla factions that are resorting to violence to impose an alternative to the dictatorship.

El Salvador can be seen as a desperate experiment on a chronically ill patient. If a remedy can be concocted, it may cure the social, economic, and political disease that is endemic in Latin America. The United States is trying hard to find the correct combination of medicines. Land reform, if successfully carried out, might break the wealth and land monopoly of the upper class. Democracy, though awkward and ineffective in its infancy, might eventually allow social justice to prevail. Military training and reform might make armed forces more of a threat to guerrillas and less of a danger to civilians and elected governments. Finally, firm military pressure from the United States may discourage the "exportation" of revolution from Cuba and its allies, and negotiations may become a more common alternative to violence.

Certainly no miracle cures for El Salvador have been found. Progress has been excruciatingly slow. Meanwhile, Honduras, which borders on El Salvador, and Guatemala, less than 100 miles (160 km) away, have been experimenting with solutions to their own similar problems and wondering whether their fate will resemble that of El Salvador.

GUATEMALA

Guatemala may be the most important country between Panama and Mexico. Its population of over 7 million is the largest in the region, its economy is the most powerful, and U.S. investment is the highest in the region—about $221 million. Most U.S. investments are in land and agricultural development. As in El Salvador, most of the wealth is confined to a small upper class. Just 2 percent of the people own two-thirds of the land. The largest landowners are foreign fruit companies. Geographically strategic, Guatemala borders on four countries, including Mexico, and has newly discovered oil fields within its territory. Over the last thirty years, United States influence in Guatemala has ranged from direct, heavy-handed interference to a righteous, hands-off refusal to become involved.

AN AMERICAN COUP

In 1954, the U.S. Central Intelligence Agency (CIA) engineered the ouster of Guatemala's liberal president Colonel Jacobo Arbenz. Arbenz had been the first president in over a century to be legally elected to office and to begin his term of office on the appointed day. His policies also marked a major change in Guatemalan life. Labor organizations were encouraged, political parties were given complete freedom, a few communists were appointed to government positions, and the press was allowed to speak out freely without fear.

Apparently President Arbenz went too far, however, when he decreed that the government intended to force the United Fruit Company to sell 178,000 of its unused acres. Measured against the 1980 American-inspired land reform in El Salvador, this was not a radical program. Arbenz considered the land reform necessary because only 2½ percent of the population owned 70 percent of the arable land in Guatemala. United Fruit was—and still is—the largest single landowner in Guatemala. Government payment for the United Fruit property was to equal the amount at which the company itself had assessed the land for tax purposes.

According to *Bitter Fruit*, a book by journalists Stephen Schlesinger and Stephen Kinzer, the United Fruit Company had powerful friends in Washington—powerful enough to convince the U.S. government to react to Arbenz's social reform program. Secretary of State John Foster Dulles said Arbenz was instituting a "communist-type reign of terror." Military aid was increased for neighboring countries while it was cut off for Guatemala.

In 1954, the CIA carried out a coup that involved U.S. pilots in U.S. planes dropping bombs on Guatemalan government buildings. When Guatemalan army officers bribed by the CIA refused to support their president, Arbenz had to flee the country.

Secretary Dulles called the coup "a new and glorious chapter" in the history of the western world.

Carlos Castillo Armas, described as "sincerely anti-communist," was installed as president. The land reform was cancelled, political parties were outlawed, labor unions were smashed, and "communism" was thoroughly wiped out.

The incident was more than just another military coup in another Central American "banana republic." Throughout Latin America, it was seen as one more example of the United States using its power to control the politics of smaller countries.

RUTHLESS REPRESSION AND REBORN REBELLION

During the next twenty-six years, the military government of Guatemala kept order through deadly force. When guerrilla activity flared up in the early 1960s—not long after the Cuban revolution—the United States sent army advisors and Green Berets of the Special Forces to help train the Guatemalan armed forces. Antiguerrilla tactics became a wholesale terrorizing of the rural population. The campaign was successful, but in 1980, a U.S. State Department study reported that "to eliminate a few hundred guerrillas, the government killed perhaps 10,000 Guatemalan peasants." By the end of the 1960s leftist activity was completely extinguished.

There was little change in Guatemala's political structure. A fraudulent election in 1974 defeated General Efraín Ríos Montt, a political moderate who was advocating a lessening of the repression of the lower class. A radical rightist general became president and gave liberals no choice but to go "underground" or die. Those who chose the former survived and had little choice but to form another guerrilla movement.

The return of leftist guerrillas has been attributed to

three factors: the new social attitudes of the Catholic church, the involvement of Guatemalan Indians, and the uprisings in Nicaragua and El Salvador.

The Catholic Church began preaching that heaven was not the only place where people could be happy, that God did not expect His children to suffer during their lives on Earth. Missionaries from around the world came to Guatemala to help solve the health, farming, and illiteracy problems of the poor. For this, many of them, including an American, were murdered by death squads. The Maryknoll Order of the Catholic Church withdrew all its missionaries in 1981, and in that same year the government said it would not be responsible for the deaths of Jesuit priests who did not leave immediately.

Indians, who make up just over half the population, traditionally kept outside of politics. As descendents of the ancient Mayas, they rejected Spanish culture, and this rejection and the preservation of their own ways have made them almost like a country within a country. Their religion is a combination of Catholic doctrine and local cults. Over twenty different languages are spoken among the Indians. During the late 1970s, the leftist insurgents realized that without the support of the Indians, they could never succeed. By teaching the Indians to read and write and then educating them (or, from the rightist point of view, brainwashing them) about their needless poverty and the injustices of their government, the leftists enlisted both the direct and the indirect support of the Indians. Today there is reported to be one guerrilla faction made up entirely of Indians, and another that is 75 percent Indians.

Since peasants, especially Indians, often contribute to the leftist effort by supplying guerrillas with food and shelter, they are often the victims of military reprisal. When guerrilla activity is reported in or around a particular village, the army may punish innocent civilians. In a few cases, the entire population of a village has been slaughtered. In 1981 and 1982, an estimated 20,000 people died this way. Less than 10 percent were armed guerrillas. This strategy of terror is intended not only to discourage peasant support of guerrillas but also to keep guerrillas away from populated areas. Theoretically, the guerrillas are supposed to realize that their presence, benevolent or not, means death to civilians.

In earlier years, Indians and others of the lower class never fought back against the injustices of their government. But the successful revolution in Nicaragua and the continuing strength of rebels in El Salvador proved that it was possible for the oppressed to rise up against their oppressors. This encouraged many of the lower class to join the revolution.

With 20,000 soldiers, the Guatemalan army is considered the best-trained and best-equipped army in Central America, except perhaps for the recently built-up Sandinista army of Nicaragua. Between 1950 and 1977, the United States was responsible for much of this power. During that time, 3,334 Guatemalan officers received training in U.S. military academies. Soldiers were equipped with American weapons, helicopters, and trucks. This was part of a policy that offered aid to virtually any government, good or bad, that was loyal to the United States.

In 1978, President Carter declared that because of its severe abuse of human rights, Guatemala was ineligible for U.S. aid and would not even be allowed to buy U.S. arms. This policy was applied to several countries around the world in hopes of coercing them to respect human rights. General Romeo Lucas García, then president of Guatemala, said his country could fight communism better without the moral restrictions placed on it by the United States. Over the next

This Guatemalan Indian and his daughter are living
in a government-sponsored refugee camp
where they hope to escape the terror directed
against Guatemala's Indian population.

three years, Guatemala spent $89 million on arms, mostly from Israel and Argentina. No longer dependent on U.S. aid, General Lucas waged war without restraint. Anyone not of the extreme right was a target for death squads. The foreign minister and the mayor of Guatemala City were among the murdered, as were seventy-six other party leaders. Even the vice president eventually fled the country.

As the election in Guatemala approached in 1982, the Reagan administration offered $3.2 million in jeeps and spare parts for helicopters to entice General Lucas to nominate a civilian for president. Ignoring the offer, the government had another general nominated and elected.

The elected president never took office, however. In April 1982, two thousand army troops surrounded the National Palace and the National Congress. The group of junior officers who organized the coup said that they and the rest of Guatemala were tired of the corruption in their government. They replaced General Lucas with General Efraín Ríos Montt, the born-again Christian who had been denied his elected office in 1974.

General Ríos announced that he would wipe out both the leftist threat and the rightist death squads with a program he called "Rifles and Beans." It began with a general amnesty for any guerrillas who turned themselves in. None did. On July 1, 1982, Ríos declared a state of siege, which cancelled all political rights indefinitely. The armed forces went to selected villages that had been identified as supporting the guerrillas and massacred their entire populations. Then, in neighboring areas, food was distributed and civil construction was begun.

Within six months, between 3,000 and 5,000 Indians died, 250,000 were made homeless, and 80,000 were forced to join civilian paramilitary patrols. Unknown numbers were tried and condemned to death by secret courts. Guerrilla activity came to a dead stop. Although Amnesty International, Americas Watch, and other human rights groups reported the brutal massacres, President Reagan said that there had been no such slaughters of innocents and that Guatemala had received a "bum rap." Reagan then lifted the arms embargo, agreeing to sell Guatemala $6.3 million in U.S. military equipment.

But had the fighting really finished? Representatives of Americas Watch interviewed dozens of Guatemalan refugees in southern Mexico. They reported that the army was continuing its efforts to kill everyone remotely involved with the rebels. The reason for an execution could be something as simple as the absence of the man of the house—a clue that he might be a guerrilla. That would put even neighbors under suspicion and therefore liable to be killed. Much of the rural population had little choice but to join the guerrillas or flee.

Americas Watch reported that between 70,000 and 100,000 Indians had escaped to refugee camps in Mexico. To arrive there, they had to cross a "free-fire" zone in which anyone would be shot on sight. Once in Mexico, they were restricted to twenty-seven camps along the border. Occasionally, Guatemalan squads crossed the border to kill suspects in the camps. A political scientist in Mexico City warned of increased border friction, because Mexico's acceptance of the refugees might be interpreted as a condemnation of Guatemala's brutal policies. To avoid problems, Mexico moved many of the camps further inside its borders.

In August 1983, General Ríos was ousted by yet another military coup, the sixth since 1954. The new president was yet another military leader, General Oscar Humberto Mejía Victores, who had been and

continued to be minister of defense. The coup, carried out with the full support of all the armed forces, was further evidence that little had changed over the century and a half of Guatemala's independence. Leadership was still determined by whoever could muster the most political and military support.

When General Mejía first took office, he made two announcements that were cautiously applauded in Washington. He promised to hold elections and discontinue the censorship of secret trials that his predecessor had imposed. He also swore to vigorously combat any leftist uprisings. He had already demonstrated his enthusiasm for the latter promise as minister of defense. Despite an earlier incident in which the army had killed two Guatemalan employees of the U.S. Agency for International Development, U.S. officials expected the general to be very cooperative with United States policies in the region. In fact, within two weeks Mejía had made arrangements with El Salvador to train some of its soldiers in counterinsurgency tactics in exchange for some of the weapons that El Salvador had received from the United States.

GUATEMALA'S FUTURE

What is Guatemala's future? No land reforms or extensive social progress are currently under consideration. There have been no substantive changes within the armed forces that might lead to a permanent end to the brutalities against civilians. The primary causes of the rebellion are still there. A lull in

**Guatemala's president,
General Oscar Humberto Mejía**

the fighting may be only a low point in a continuing cycle of violence and calm. While Guatemala claims to be one of the few countries in recent history to defeat a guerrilla army, it may only be in the eye of the Central American hurricane. Many Guatemalans are hoping their government will use this calm to make the social reforms that might prevent another uprising, but such programs are not likely to be carried out.

The United States could not afford to let Guatemala fall to communist forces. It would be seen as the last domino before Mexico. The jungle-covered mountains of Guatemala would be ideal places from which to launch guerrilla forays into Mexico and Honduras. Newly discovered oil fields in Guatemala as well as those of southern Mexico would be valuable territory worth fighting for. Both Mexico and Honduras suffer the problems of severe poverty, which make them highly susceptible to revolutionary uprisings. How susceptible Guatemala will be to rebellion, and how much it will deserve U.S. aid to fight those rebellions, will depend on whether it manages to move toward democracy and social justice for the lower class.

Neighboring Honduras and Costa Rica may be good examples of how poor Central American countries can break with a tradition of military government, maintain a basic if flawed respect for human rights, and make genuine efforts to create a democracy. One effect of this progress has been excellent relations with the United States. Another has been a noteworthy lack of violence from the left. While the world wonders whether Guatemalan politics will ever catch up with the twentieth century, Honduras is already struggling to make the transition from dictatorship to democracy, and Costa Rica has established a stable, long-standing tradition of democracy and peace.

HONDURAS AND COSTA RICA

Honduras has been spared extensive civil unrest, but the explosive elements of rebellion are strong. The three million people of Honduras have the lowest per capita income in Central America—about $540 per year. Unemployment stands at 22 percent, and about the same percent have only part-time or seasonal work. Almost half the people are illiterate. Agriculture and related industries provide 45 percent of the gross national product. As in Guatemala, multinational corporations own a great deal of the farmland. As in El Salvador, a fragile newborn democracy holds only loose reins on a free-willed military. With borders on Nicaragua, El Salvador, and Guatemala, Honduras may be inevitably destined to a future of violence.

UNITED STATES AID

While its neighbors have been disqualified or barely qualified for U.S. military aid, Honduras has received amounts that have tripled every year for three years—$3.5 million in 1980, $10 million in 1981, and over $31 million in 1982. In 1983, President Reagan asked Congress to approve $76 million.

The United States has also provided economic aid to stave off bankruptcy. Income from exported bananas and coffee has not kept up with the cost of imported oil. In 1983, with Honduras owing $75 million to foreign banks and the economy dropping at a rate of 1.2% per year, the United States sent $98.6 million in economic aid.

DEMOCRACY UNDER PRESSURE

Honduras has been the recipient of such consistent aid because it has maintained a consistently cooperative relationship with the United States. In the past, its military government remained strongly anticommunist while showing more respect for human rights than most Central American governments. The United States also wanted to help an eager new democracy in the region. Elections for a constituent assembly in 1980 drew voters in record numbers. In 1981, honest presidential elections installed Roberto Suazo Córdova, a civilian, as the country's democratic leader. The United States felt this was a political situation worth investing in.

There is much concern, however, that the real leader of Honduras is General Gustavo Alvarez Martinez. As commander-in-chief of the armed forces, Alvarez has the power, if not the authority, to fight leftist subversion without regard for constitutional law. Because of increasing U.S. military involvement in Honduras, critics of General Alvarez claim that his power could get out of control. So far, Córdova says that Alvarez obeys orders, and Alvarez recognizes that it would be a crime against his country not to respect the duly elected representatives in Tegucigalpa.

There have been indications, however, that the armed forces are acting outside the law. According to the Honduran Commission for the Defense of Human Rights, thirty-four political activists were murdered in 1982 and five others disappeared in suspicious circumstances. In April 1983, a death squad gunned down three labor union leaders. The murderers in the latter case, however, were quickly put on trial.

This level of violence by no means approaches the levels found in El Salvador and Guatemala. But the outrage that some groups of citizens have expressed could build up into a force that touches off an explosive rebellion. Already several small guerrilla organizations have formed. One, the Chinchoneros Popular Liberation Movement, hijacked a plane and held a hundred business people and government officials hostage for several days. Police have also discovered several caches of weapons in Tegucigalpa. The arms came from Cuba and were probably bound for El Salvador.

U.S. Ambassador to Honduras John Negroponte says that the idea that the Honduran military rules the country is just an erroneously stereotypical view of a Central American country. Local business and civic leaders say, however, that the military is in control simply because the elected government is so inefficient. Rather than deal with overwhelming bureaucracy, they prefer to ask General Alvarez to give a few orders and get things done.

REFUGEES

Since Honduras has remained in relative peace while wars have raged around it, refugees have fled there from all sides. From Nicaragua came over 20,000 people, many of them Miskito Indians and the families of the contra rebels. Another 20,000 came from El Salvador. Smaller numbers came from Guatemala.

These homeless people, whose numbers increase daily, have been confined to the border areas. Honduras is offering them temporary asylum, not permanent residence. So they survive in tents and huts, eating inadequate food supplies donated by the United Nations, the Organization of American States, and church groups. There have been many accusations that much of this food ends up in the hands of Salvadoran guerrillas. Several times the Salvadoran armed forces have crossed the border to search refugee camps for alleged guerrillas who were seeking asylum and supplies. But as one priest there explained, "How could people who have so little give anything away?"

THE *CONTRA* INVASION

Since 1979, Honduras has been concerned about the military build-up in Nicaragua. General Alvarez said that Nicaragua's army was as big as the combined forces of all other Central American countries. While Nicaragua certainly feared invasion from its neighbors, the build-up was seen by those countries as a possible preparation for an attack against one or more of them. Distrust of the Sandinistas contributed to Honduran military cooperation with the United States and the contra rebels. The Honduran army has been helping the contras train and prepare for their invasion. In Nicaragua, contra camps are within 10 miles (16 km) of the border. Although Honduras says its troops stay far from the border, Nicaragua claims that Hondurans have provided cover fire for invading contras and have prevented Nicaragua from pursuing the contras when they retreat into Honduran territory. Honduras has reminded Nicaragua that the Sandinistas had the same help and protection when they were using Honduran territory to launch attacks against Somoza.

Reacting to these raids and retreats, Nicaraguan Defense Minister Humberto Ortega Saavedra has threatened to invade Honduras in order to protect his territory. He also called on Honduran leftists to attack *contra* bases. While these threats were generally seen as nothing more than bold words, they hint at how rapidly a full-scale regional war could spread across Central America. Some political analysts have suggested that the CIA is tempting the Nicaraguans to attack so that greater U.S. involvement can be justified. If war did break out between Honduras and Nicaragua, the United States would be expected to back the 11,500 Honduran soldiers who would face up to 25,000 Nicaraguans.

THE AMERICAN PRESENCE

In May 1983, the White House announced plans to set up a military base in northern Honduras on the Caribbean coast. Staffed by about 125 U.S. military advisors, it would be used to train Salvadoran soldiers. Many Hondurans expressed concern about this, however. They had fought a short border war with El Salvador in 1969 and still distrusted that country. Hondurans also questioned the way the agreement between the United States and El Salvador had been worked out. The Honduran constitution calls for the approval of the assembly before foreign troops can be stationed on Honduran soil. President Suazo Córdova and the assembly, however, had had nothing to do with the decision. General Alvarez had made all the arrangements without consulting the proper officials. Using a technicality to circumvent the law, he declared that the Salvadorans would be referred to as students, not troops. His disregard for legal channels and the intent of the law reminded everyone that, ultimately, the military held the real power in Honduras.

Honduras became an even stronger bastion of U.S.

policies in Central America with the advent of the Big Pine II operations. The presence of 5,000 U.S. military personnel clearly signaled to Nicaragua and Cuba that American forces were welcome in Honduras and that leftist forces were not. As a democracy that was surviving amid poverty, Honduras would be protected as a showcase of what was possible in Central America without Cuban intervention or leftist uprisings.

Some political analysts, however, question the wisdom of too much military aid to a country with such a weak, unpracticed democracy. Central American history has shown repeatedly that democracies do not last long where the military has traditionally held power and office. The only democracy that has lived long enough to become traditional is that of Costa Rica. And it has done so without an army.

COSTA RICA: PEACE, PROSPERITY, AND PROBLEMS

Although very significant in its unique position in Central America, Costa Rica belongs as a footnote in a book on revolution. Having become a democracy in 1948 and having abolished its army a year later, Costa Rica is proud of what it does not have. There are no death squads, no political prisoners, no restrictions on freedom, no landed oligarchy, no hunger, and no guerrilla war.

This is not to say that Costa Rica has no problems. The economy is in serious trouble. Per capita income, although by far the highest in the region, has dropped from $1,800 per annum to less than $1,300. The total foreign debt is over $4 billion. The country cannot even afford to pay the interest on the loans it must take to pay debtors. International money-lending institutions such as the World Bank are demanding cuts in public spending for the country to qualify for more loans. As public services are reduced, the citizenry becomes less satisfied with the government.

And due to its stability, relative prosperity, and neutral position, Costa Rica is becoming a haven for refugees. The government, trying to avoid taking sides in the conflicts of its neighbors to the north, accepts all refugees with legitimate need for asylum. As greater numbers arrive, the economic burden becomes heavier. Estimates of the number of refugees reach as high as 200,000—about a tenth of the country's native population.

The refugees, who are rightist and leftist exiles from Nicaragua, El Salvador, Guatemala, and Cuba, bring political tension to San José, the capital. Caches of arms, probably bound for Nicaragua or El Salvador, have been found. There have been a few kidnappings, bombings, and assassinations, all involving foreigners acting against foreigners.

Despite these problems, Costa Rica steadfastly insists on democracy and neutrality. When U.S. Senator Charles Percy offhandedly remarked that, in the face of so much turmoil in the region, Costa Rica should perhaps build an army, the public outcry was loud and indignant. One columnist said that that would be "a solution more dangerous than the problem."

TOWARD PEACE

Peace will come neither quickly nor easily to Central America. It is highly unlikely that any of the many conflicting forces will achieve a final and complete military victory. There also seems little possibility that massive foreign aid or investment will be offered to alleviate the poverty of the area. Political repression and civil unrest will probably continue as long as there are rightists and leftists with no democratic or negotiating process through which they can settle their differences.

Many leaders and political analysts feel that the only solution is to have the conflicting parties agree to stop fighting and start talking and listening to each other. Perhaps at the negotiating table they can understand each other's problems, resolve their differences, and agree on constructive solutions. That, of course, is easy to say and virtually impossible to do. But a few cautious steps have been taken.

In October 1982, the United States organized the Conference of Democratic Nations in San José, Costa

Rica. The members of the conference endorsed a withdrawal of all foreign troops and advisors from Central America, the banning of heavy weapons from the area, an end to all insurgencies, and the establishment of democratic governments. The agreement was hopelessly optimistic, however. Since neither Nicaragua, Cuba, nor any leftist groups had been included in the talks, the words stood little chance of becoming actions.

In January 1983, a slightly more realistic meeting was held on the Panamanian island of Contadora. Representatives from Mexico, Venezuela, Panama, and Colombia met and agreed to help organize talks among all nations and all conflicting parties in Central America. While recognizing that settlement would be difficult if not impossible to arrange, the Contadora group felt that the only hope was to include everyone in the process of searching for peace. The group planned a meeting for representatives from Costa Rica, Honduras, Guatemala, El Salvador, and Nicaragua. The United States, although not invited, expressed support for the idea of Latin Americans solving their own problems through negotiations.

In April 1983, representatives of the nine countries met in Panama, though they could not agree to sit at the same table. The following month, the foreign ministers of those countries met, talked, and agreed to recommend an end to the militarization of the area and the opening of dialogues between opposing parties. The most urgent dialogue was to be between Nicaragua and Honduras, both of which were warning that they were on the brink of war.

When Special Envoy Richard Stone returned to Washington in June 1983 after an eleven-day tour through ten Central American and Caribbean countries, he recommended that Washington fully support the Contadora proposal. He said that since this was

Presidents of the countries
that comprise the Contadora group
sit down to lunch with their aides
after a meeting in Cancún, Mexico.
The presidents are, from left,
Colombia's Belisario Betancur,
Venezuela's Luís Herrera Campins,
Mexico's Miguel de la Madrid, and
Panama's Ricardo de la Espriella.

the only initiative in progress, it was the best hope for averting widespread disaster in the region.

The presidents of the four countries in the Contadora group proposed several points that, if agreed upon even in part, would bring the region much closer to peace. They recommended pacts of nonaggression; a halt to all arms shipments into and among the nations involved; negotiations for arms reductions; a prohibition against foreign military bases, troops and advisors; and better communications among leaders.

Formulating such proposals is, of course, much easier than achieving them. But they are points that are ripe for discussion, a starting place slightly closer to the final goal of peace. In fact, within a few weeks of the Contadora group's announcement of the proposals, Nicaraguan leader Daniel Ortega Saavedra said that his country was prepared to unilaterally accept all parts of the plan. Cuba, too, expressed a willingness to remove its advisors from Nicaragua and end arms shipments if the United States would do the same regarding El Salvador. But the quick cooperation of the two socialist countries was not entirely due to an urge for peace. They were, at that time, feeling immense pressure from the American Big Pine II operations. Also, by that time, Nicaragua needed Cuban and Soviet assistance less than El Salvador and Honduras needed United States assistance. Strategically, the socialist countries would have come out ahead in any multilateral acceptance of the Contadora proposal.

Reactions among the Central American countries varied. Honduras and Guatemala wanted to continue putting pressure on Nicaragua, perhaps to the point of toppling the Sandinistas. Mexico and Costa Rica took a more moderate stance, accepting the principles of the Contadora proposal. José Napoleon Duarte, former president of El Salvador and at that time a candidate in the 1984 elections, said he opposed Nicaragua's interference in his country but admitted that "Nicaraguans have a right to their own revolution." Meanwhile, Daniel Ortega went on record as saying that Nicaragua's revolution was the beginning of Central America's revolution. The conflicting opinions illustrated the improbability of a settlement in the near future.

Opinions in Washington were no more unanimous than in Central America. Democrats, following the guidance of Senator Christopher Dodd, inevitably questioned President Reagan's semiannual certifications of improvements in the human rights situation in El Salvador. Progress toward negotiations with the FDR was a subject raised several times. In the debate over support for the contras in Nicaragua, Congressmen Edward Boland and Clement Zablocki led Democrats in an attempt to cut off funding.

Regarding the Big Pine II maneuvers, again opinions were split along party lines, with the Democrats most concerned that the possibility of regional talks had been replaced by a gunboat diplomacy that threatened to touch off a regional war. The likelihood of increasing aid to Guatemala was also debated following the coup that put General Mejía in power.

With so many points being questioned, debated, and criticized, President Reagan was having a difficult time putting together a policy that would receive broad support in the government and among the public. In hopes of reducing current controversy and producing a more widely accepted future policy, he appointed a bipartisan commission to study the problems of Central America. The twelve-member commission would then make recommendations for long-term United States policies.

The commission was designed to reduce controversy by being balanced with Republicans and Democrats and community leaders who owed no political allegiance to any party. Among the members were Robert S. Strauss, chairperson of President Carter's reelection campaign; Joseph Lane Kirkland, president of the AFL-CIO; Potter Stewart, retired Supreme Court justice; Dr. William Walsh, founder and president of Project Hope; and Carlos F. Diaz-Alejandro, a professor of economics at Yale University who was born in Havana, Cuba.

Predictably, there was controversy over how balanced the commission was, whether it was just a political maneuver aimed at validating the president's policies, and whether Mr. Diaz-Alejandro was biased in his opinions on Cuba. Most controversial of all, however, was President Reagan's choice for chairperson of the commission—former Secretary of State Henry Kissinger. Although President Reagan had once criticized Dr. Kissinger in the past, he felt that this highly experienced international diplomat was "the right man for the job." Furthermore, he was a household name well known for establishing diplomatic relations with China, negotiating an end to the war in Vietnam, easing tension in the Middle East, and reaching an agreement on nuclear arms limitations with the Soviet Union.

Some of Dr. Kissinger's policies as Secretary of State, however, were widely criticized and, according to many, antithetical to the goals of the commission. In 1970, when Salvador Allende, a socialist, was elected President of Chile, Secretary Kissinger commented, "I don't see why we need to stand by and watch a country go communist due to the irresponsibility of its own people." Journalists later implicated him and the CIA in the military coup that overthrew and killed Salvador Allende. Dr. Kissinger is also widely criticized for blaming all too many local problems on the global struggle between the United States and the Soviet Union. He subscribes to the "balance of power" theory that holds that one way to secure peace is to let opposing sides maintain equal military power. How these previous experiences and political opinions would affect the commission's report were of great concern to Congress and the Senate.

President Reagan asked the commission to formulate its recommendations by December 1983, but Chairperson Kissinger said it would take until February 1984. Meanwhile, the Contadora group said that the situation could not wait that long. No one, however, expected either group to achieve any immediate effects on conditions in Central America. Before the commission could reach a fundamental consensus on which to base its decisions, it would have to consider dozens of policy options. The Contadora group would have to find a miraculous formula that would somehow satisfy the many different countries, armies, leaders, and parties. And if either managed to produce a reasonable program or policy, it would probably take ten or twenty years to end all vestiges of conflict.

Few consider such a time frame unlikely. The problems in Central America are too deeply rooted in the past and too tightly interconnected with gobal politics to be corrected by a fleet of ships, an infusion of money, or the good intentions of neutral negotiators. As long as hunger, disease, ignorance, greed, revenge, fear, distrust, and despair remain, the fighting is bound to continue.

FOR FURTHER READING

El Salvador: Central America in the New Cold War (Edited by Marvin Gettleman et al., New York: Grove Press, 1981) is an excellent collection of articles by over fifty knowledgeable political analysts and officials. For a view somewhat biased toward the left, read the several articles and documents reproduced in *Revolution and Intervention in Central America*, by Marlene Dixon and Susanne Jonas, a lengthy edition of a journal published by Synthesis Publication (San Francisco, 1981). *The Cuban Threat*, by Carla Anne Robbins (New York: McGraw-Hill, 1982) is a well-researched and unbiased report on Cuban activities in Latin America. *El Salvador: Country In Crisis*, by Glenn Alan Cheney (New York: Franklin Watts, 1982) gives a thorough background on the history of El Salvador and the early years of its current crisis.

For truly up-to-date information on the rapidly changing events in Latin America, it is necessary to read such periodicals as *Time, Newsweek, Foreign Policy, Foreign Affairs, Latin America Weekly Report,* and reputable newspapers.

INDEX

Dodd, Senator Christopher, 55–56, 84
Donovan, Jean, 49
Duarte, President José Napoléon, 40–42, 44, 48, 53, 54, 83–84
Dulles, John Foster, 63

Enders, Thomas O., 58

Farabundo Marti, Agustín, 37
FDN, 27, 29–30
FDR, 47–48, 52–53, 57, 60, 84
Federation of Central America, 5
FMLN, 47
Ford, Ita, 49
FSLN, 17–18

García, José, 42, 58

Haig, Alexander, 24, 26–27, 50
Hammer, Mike, 44
Hinton, Dean, 58

John Paul II (pope), 30, 31, 32
Johnson, President Lyndon B., 52

Kazel, Dorothy, 49
Kennedy, President John F., 10
Kissinger, Dr. Henry, 85–86
Krushchev, Premier Nikita, 10

Latin American Episcopal Conference, 1968, 8
Legal Aid Commission, 40, 48
Lucas García, General Romeo, 66, 68

Magaña, President Alvaro, 53, 54, 57
Mejía Victores, General Oscar Humberto, 69, 70, 71, 84
Mexico, 5, 14–15, 62, 69, 72, 81, 83
Miskito Indians, 26, 75
Mondale, Walter, 59

Negroponte, John, 75

ORDEN, 40–41
Organization of American States, 76
Ortega Saavedra, Daniel, 23, 31, 32–33, 83–84
Ortega Saavedra, Humberto, 23, 77

Pastora Gomez, Edén, 17–18, 23, 28, 29
Pearlman, Mark, 44
Percy, Senator Charles, 79
Project Hope, 85

Reagan, President Ronald, 2, 24–26, 29, 32–35, 49–50, 53, 60, 68–69, 74, 84–86
Ríos Montt, General Efraín, 64, 68–69
Robelo Calejas, Alfonso, 22–23, 29
Roman Catholic Church, 7–8, 22, 30, 40, 48, 65
Romero, President Carlos Humberto, 41
Romero, Archbishop Oscar Arnulfo, 40–41, 53

Sandinistas, 17–19, 20, 21–23, 26–29, 34–35, 41, 49, 60, 66, 76, 83
Sandino, Augusto César, 14–15, 17, 37
Schlesinger, Stephen, 63
Shultz, Secretary of State George, 35, 58
Somoza, Anastasio "Tacho," 14–15
Somoza Debayle, President Anastasio "Tachito," 15–19, 23–24, 29, 35, 41, 45, 76
Somoza, Luis, 15
Soviet Union, 1–4, 8–11, 19, 22–25, 34–35, 48, 50, 52
Stone, Richard, 32–33, 57, 60, 81